CROSS-COUNTRY SKIING
IN ONTARIO

IRIS NOWELL

Illustrations by John Ward

Art Director Ron Butler
Research Assistant Lesley Hailstone

The assistance of the following people is gratefully acknowledged:
Birley Cowan, Bruce Trail Association
Mike Exall, Outdoor Recreation Co-Ordinator, Seneca College, King
Campus, Director of Wilderness Training
Malcolm Hunter, Southern Ontario Junior Team Coach, former Olympic
(1972) National Team member
Lembit Joselin, coach, Canadian Ski Association
David Margesson, Margesson Sporting Goods
Neil MacDonald, Southern Ontario Ski Division, Canadian Ski Association
representative
Ian Micklethwaite, Ontario Cross-Country Ski Association representative
Erling Morris, CSI, Norwegian Ski Shop

CONTENTS

HISTORY

Until the late 1960s, the Scandinavians and Central Europeans had cross-country skiing in North America all to themselves. Then came the boom. In the past few years there has been little to equal the enthusiasm for cross-country. Even those who predicted an awakening interest have been astounded by the thousands upon thousands of newcomers eagerly pursuing the sport.

On reflection, the boom is not surprising. Of all mass interest sports, cross-country skiing appeals to countless tastes and meets today's priorities head on. It's the ideal family outing. It's economical. And for fitness and conditioning no popular sport can match it. Numerous downhillers, weary of increasing expenses and long lineups, are making the switch to cross-country, and campers, canoeists and back-packers have found the sport an ideal extension of their summer activities. Add to this the growing numbers of normally unathletic people who merely wish peaceful escape from city noise, traffic and crowds, and cross-country has proven to be an enjoyable winter activity for just about everyone. No wonder the sport is booming.

Wherever snow has carpeted the earth there has been some means of quickly travelling over it. Carvings on rocks depict skiing as transportation in hunting and war as far back as 4,000 years ago, and skis (believed to be the first ever used) recovered from Swedish bogs also date from the same period. Although Norse mythology has been dominated by stirring legends of the sea, mention of skis can also be found, and by the 10th and 11th Centuries it was definitely established that they were used as a means of transportation in Viking wars. Ancient woodcuts portray these early skis as short and broad, with animal furs on the bottom to provide traction. In the course of their evolution, skis have taken many forms. Perhaps the most improbable were those used during the 17th Century —one ski was very long, the other much shorter.

By the 12th Century skiing began its transition from a means of survival to a sport, although at that time it was a sport pursued only by royalty. Not until the 16th and 17th Centuries did the transition reach the common folk, and this occurred primarily because of the military. Competitions were a natural outgrowth of military training pro-

Skiing in 1678

4

grams, and when civilians noticed these lusty sporting events, they wanted to join in.

Scandinavian history is full of heroic deeds of skiers in battle. In 1206, the Norwegian two-year-old King, Haakon IV, was rescued from the enemy by two swift skiers who raced the infant to safety over the mountains.

In 1521, Swedish patriot Gustaf Vasa led his countrymen in an attack which freed them from the rule of the Danes and was thereupon crowned King of Sweden. From the victory comes today's most celebrated cross-country event, the Vasaloppet first held in 1921 to re-trace the King's 400-year old journey through the forests of Dalarna. Now, the over-85 kilometre race attracts as many as 10,000 competitors and is the largest ski race in the world.

By the early 1700s, cross-country skiing was firmly ensconced in the sporting lifestyle of the Norwegians, and by the beginning of the 19th Century, emigrating Scandinavians were introducing their sport to New Englanders and Eastern Canadians. It was appropriate; there was no end of suitable terrain in the "new land".

One of the early skiing heroes of America was John "Snowshoe" Thompson, a Norwegian immigrant who skied the U.S. mails from California to Nevada in the 1850s. There have been many notables since, but of all the contemporary heroes and personalities in cross-country skiing, probably the most colourful is Quebec's Herman "Jack Rabbit" Johannsen. Almost single-handedly he put the Laurentians on the map. He blazed trails, organized competitions, designed courses, trained youngsters, was part of the development of the world's first ski tow at Shawbridge, Quebec in 1928, and in general, fired up the whole region with an undying enthusiasm for skiing. As a cross-country skier he was considered remarkable in his mid-60s. In 1975 he celebrates his 100th year by (what else!) skiing.

It was the 1932 Winter Olympics in Lake Placid, New York and rapid expansion of lifts and tows that changed the entire focus of skiing in North America. Once it became possible to ride thousands of feet to the top of a mountain and swoosh down in a matter of minutes, and then go up and do it all over again, "downhill" became the glamour sport. By comparison, cross-country seemed lacklustre. Interest in the sport was kept alive only by a few diehards—until the '70s when the pendulum began its new swing.

what is
CROSS-COUNTRY SKIING?

Cross-country skiing, often called ski touring, is several sports within a sport.

Each presents its own challenges and thrills, and each, happily, can be enjoyed at varying levels of competency.

Here are the common types of cross-country skiing:

Racing

Racing brings out, with equal enthusiasm, kindergarten youngsters and stout-hearted ladies and gentlemen of retirement age. Races are usually conducted over courses from one to 50 kilometres. Equipment is light weight.

Mountaineering

One of the most thrilling and challenging winter sports, mountaineering is also a specialized subject not dealt with in this book. For reference books, see page 44.

Mountaineering, predictably, is mostly done on mountain snow fields or glaciers. It is the perfect sport for hikers and back-packers who wish to extend their outdoor activities from summer to winter. Equipment is a compromise between general touring and Alpine.

Orienteering

A popular competitive sport in Scandinavian countries, it is now gaining appeal with cross-country skiers in North America. Orienteering is like car rallying in that you need compasses and maps to successfully get from checkpoint to checkpoint.

Light Touring

For Southern Ontario residents light touring has a great advantage— it can be done in very little snow. Light touring involves skiing on prepared trails or open spaces such as conservation areas, golf courses or parks. For good skiers this is fast, graceful skiing on fairly light equipment.

General Touring

General touring is cross-country skiing in wilderness areas—rugged terrain, deep snow, plenty of trees, and hills—in short, skiing well off the beaten track. Hence its other name "bushwacking". Equipment is rugged although not as heavy as that required for downhill.

CHOOSING YOUR EQUIPMENT

Because cross-country skiing is fairly new as a popular sport in North America, expertise on equipment is varied. Would-be enthusiasts can find themselves face to face with ski salesmen who are not as knowledgeable about cross-country as they are about other mass interest sports. This book will help you choose the right equipment. While the information has been gathered from recognized cross-country ski experts, their views occasionally differ. To assist you in determining what is best for you, their various opinions are included.

The first, and one of the most important shopping tips, is to find a retailer with a cross-country skier on staff. That person's help, along with what you'll learn here, should ensure that you make the right purchases.

Whatever you do, don't rush into a sporting goods shop at 5:30 on Saturday and expect to outfit the whole family for Sunday skiing. Take the time to make sound decisions, even if it means trying on every boot in the shop. Cross-country equipment can be purchased from sporting goods shops listed in the Yellow Pages under *Ski Equipment, Retail,* in sporting goods sections of department stores and at pro shops in some ski areas. If you know a few people who already ski, take advantage of their advice about where to buy.

As for price, that old dictum, you get what you pay for, aptly applies to the purchase of cross-country equipment. There are many excellent sale packages offered, but some, unfortunately, contain poor quality skis or boots. However, if you know what you're buying, you can find genuine bargains.

Expect to pay up to a total of $150.00 for the finest quality wood skis, boots, poles and bindings. A regularly-priced $70.00 to $90.00 outfit should give you good quality—and this price range is probably best for beginners. If you pay much less, that's what you'll get.

Some retailers rent equipment—they usually mention this in their ads in the Yellow Pages but a little phoning around may be necessary. In-town rental rates vary from $4.00–$5.00 with a $20.00–$25.00 deposit.

The *Where To Ski* section beginning on page 49, designates ski areas that also rent equipment. Their prices range from a high of $6.00 to $8.00 a day to a low of a few cents.

SKIS

The type of skiing you expect to do and where you'll be doing it determines the type of skis you should buy.

There are three choices:

General Touring—the heaviest most rugged ski—used mostly in heavy bush country, undulating terrain, deep snow, off the beaten track. Weight: approx. 5½ lbs.

Light Touring—lighter, thinner—for speed on prepared trails and good for fairly open spaces. Weight: approx. 4½ lbs.

Racing—the lightest, thinnest—strictly for racing. Weight: approx. 3½ lbs.

Just what is most suitable for the first-timer is one of the subjects which divides the experts. Many believe that beginners and those with co-ordination difficulties, will feel more secure on the heavier, general touring ski. Others recommend the light touring ski because of its lightness and flexibility. There is no prestige or fashion involved. Advanced skiers use both general and light touring skis, as do beginners. If you think you'll want

sturdiness, or you're attracted to the ruggedness of the bush, get general touring skis. But if it's lightness and speed you're after, light touring skis are the ones for you.

Types

Skis fall into four basic types—wood, synthetic, combinations of both and metal.

Wood—Wood skis are made of a variety of woods that are laminated as many as 32 times. The most widely used woods are birch and hickory. Birch is the lightest and holds the wax best. Hickory accepts wax well and is harder. Generally

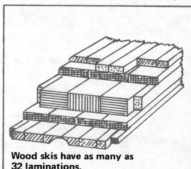

Wood skis have as many as 32 laminations.

8

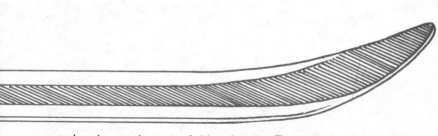

accepted as the very best wood skis (and most expensive) are hickory with lignostone edges. Lignostone is pressed, impregnated beech wood, which gives a fine, hard edge. A light wood such as birch, wears out quickly and is susceptible to breakage, so you're better off with a harder wood—like hickory—and hard edges.

Fiberglass—More expensive than wood skis, fiberglass skis offer durability and less breakage. But the problem at this time is that fiberglass is difficult to wax, especially for the beginner. However, advancing technology is making gains (see *Waxing,* page 21).

Wood and Synthetic Combinations—The bottoms of some wood skis are coated with fiberglass or various plastics which provide a tough, fast base. They require no tar treatment prior to waxing, but they don't hold wax as well as wood. Nothing developed at this time duplicates the ability of wood to hold wax. There are a number of different combinations, so be sure you know what you're getting.

Waxless—Fish Scales and Mohair—Fish scales are what the name implies. Their base is a synthetic material that looks like overlapping fish scales. A caution: this surface wears down and is not replacable. Mohair skis have two thin strips of mohair running along the base. The problem with these skis is that mohair can ice up in freezing conditions and although the strips are replacable, installation can sometimes be tricky. If you are considering mohairs, check to see that the mohair strips are sufficiently inset into base,or the skis won't grip the snow effectively. The so-called advantage of fish scales and mohairs is that you don't wax them. So these types are recommended for people who will either ski only occasionally or for those who simply can't be bothered with waxing. (Waxing, contrary to popular opinion, is not complicated. See page 21.)

Metal—Although relatively uncommon, there are some skis with a wood core and a thin aluminum "skin" covering tops and bottoms. They are fairly lightweight and rugged, with good edges. But once again, nothing holds wax better than wood.

SKIS *continued*

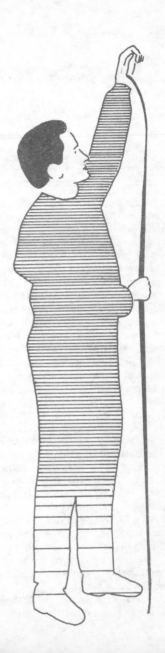

When you've determined your type of ski, length and flexibility are the next considerations.

Length
There are two commonly accepted ways of selecting the proper length of ski for your height.
Usually, skis are measured in centimetres, so a general rule of thumb is to add 30 centimetres (a foot) to your height—and that's your ski length. The other way to determine your correct length (unless you have particularly long or short arms), is to stand the ski beside you and stretch your arm straight up so the tip of the ski comes to the wrist. Most experts agree that beginners, especially those with poor co-ordination, should subtract about 5 centimetres from the prescribed length.

Children's Skis
Young children ideally should have shorter skis so they don't get them all tangled up. Yet on the practical side, if you buy skis a little bit long, they'll do for the next season as well.

Width

A certain amount of confusion can exist here because width is sometimes measured at the widest point of the ski—at the top—and sometimes at the midpoint where the ski is always narrower.

These are the approximate widths measured at the top:

General Touring—7 centimetres (approx. 3 inches)

Light Touring—6.5 centimetres (approx. 2¾ inches)

Racing—under 6 centimetres (approx. 2½ inches)

Flexibility

How "stiff" or "soft" you want your skis, depends both on your personal preference and your weight. Because flexibility is the built-in factor which distributes your weight evenly along the ski and gives the springiness that whisks you over the snow, it is very important.

Don't squeeze the skis together at the bindings to test flexibility as some will suggest. That's for experts. A more reliable test is to stand on the skis before you purchase them. Place a piece of paper under the middle of skis. If it can be pulled out easily, there is not enough flexibility for your weight. Keep trying different skis. The paper should slide out with some resistance.

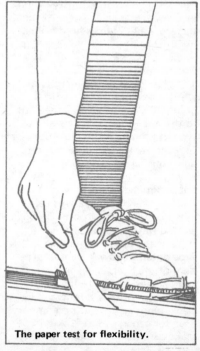

The paper test for flexibility.

BINDINGS

Of the many varieties of bindings, there are only two basic types: the toe binding and the cable binding. Both are simple, lightweight and inexpensive compared to Alpine bindings.

The action of cross-country skiing involves lifting up the heel to glide, therefore all bindings hold primarily at the toe.

Toe Binding
The plate of this binding has pins which correspond to holes in the boot and a clamp secures the boot to the ski. Called a *rat trap*, this type of binding is the most popular for both the general touring and light touring ski.

Cable Binding
With a cable binding, a stiff cable extends from a toe iron to a groove around the heel of the boot. Heavier than the toe binding, this type doesn't allow maximum freedom of the heel. It has the advantage, however, of offering a little more support, making turns easier. Cable bindings are most commonly used for general touring skis, but make sure the cable doesn't attach to lugs on the side of the ski at the heel (this type is for mountaineering, not touring).

Heel Plates
A small saw-toothed metal plate, attached to the ski where the heel of the boot touches down, helps grip the boot to keep your foot from slipping off the ski. This steadies the ski in turning and downhill running. It also prevents snow from balling under the foot. Another type is the rubber bubble, or "pop up". It merely keeps snow from balling under the foot. Heel plates are included with some bindings, but with others can be one or two dollars extra.

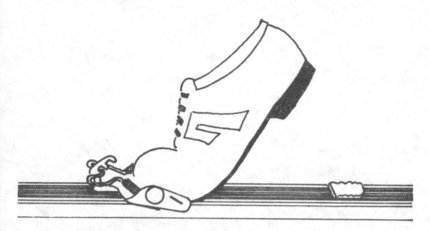

Cross-country bindings allow heel to life

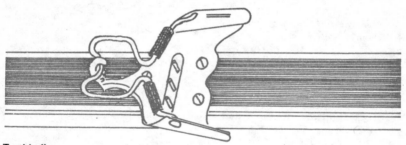

Toe binding

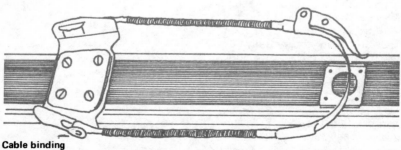

Cable binding

13

BOOTS

Boots should be selected both for the type of skiing and the type of ski. Whatever you buy, make sure your boots are fitted to your bindings to ensure compatibility.

Types
The three basic boot types correspond with the three types of skis:
- **General Touring** are rugged, the heaviest of the cross-country type, and come up over the ankle
- **Light Touring** are a little lighter, usually more flexible and come up to the ankle
- **Racing** boots are the track shoes of cross-country, are very light and are cut below the ankle

Children's Boots
It's possible to spend up to $35.00 for your five-year-old's boots, but most young children get along just fine with their ordinary snow boots. In which case, you can get an inexpensive cable-type binding with a strap that holds the toe down.

Fit
Improperly fitted boots will certainly take the fun out of cross-

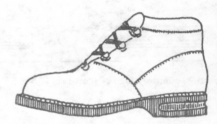

General touring

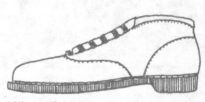

Light touring

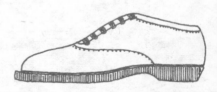

Racing

country skiing. Like any boots or shoes, they must be comfortable. Always try on boots with whatever socks you'll be wearing—generally, a light pair as well as a heavier one. With a proper fit you should be able to wiggle your toes. And your heels should be snug, otherwise you'll get blisters and your kick motion will be impaired.

Boots should flex freely at the ball of the foot. Check this by holding down the toe of your boot and pushing the heel up.

Now try twisting the boot. If it twists too easily it is not sturdy enough, and this will cause lateral movement when you ski.

You need good support under the arches. If your boots don't provide this, put in arch supports.

Synthetics vs Leather
Leather uppers are recommended because they are warm, durable and give good support. As a natural material they allow ventilation, which prevents the excess perspiration that makes feet cold.

There are many synthetic boots on the market now. They are inexpensive but bear in mind, your feet don't "breathe" in them and they don't give the support that leather does.

Another thing, some synthetics look like leather, so if you're in doubt, be sure to ask.

Soles
Some soles are leather, which requires more care, but the most common are the molded rubber or polyurethane types. Many boots you'll see have ready-made holes to fit the binding pins, others are soft enough for the pins to stick into. If you have to drill holes in your boots, this is a minor operation. But it must be accurate, so you should probably ask your retailer to do it.

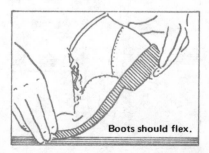

Boots should flex.

15

POLES

Cross-country ski poles are light and springy, and a good selection is available at a low price.

Types
The most widely-used poles are made of bamboo; it has the desired characteristics of strength, light weight and liveliness. Over the past two or three years metal and fiberglass poles meeting these same specifications have been put on the market. These are less likely to break—which may justify their extra cost.

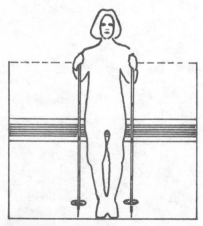

Length
It's easy to determine the proper length of your poles. Standing in a relaxed position, tuck both poles under your armpits. When the tops fit right into the armpits, that's likely to be your length. Slightly longer poles are preferred by some skiers, so the rule is, poles should come somewhere between the armpit and the shoulder.

Baskets
There are only slight differences in the size of baskets, but if you plan to be bushwacking in deep snow, choose the largest.

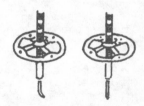

Pole Tips
Cross-country pole tips are traditionally bent, so that they will pull out of the snow quickly. But this is not critical. The straight-up tip is satisfactory for most skiers, especially beginners.

ACCESSORIES

No need to remind you that sports shops are filled with enticing extras in varying degrees of usefulness. The items described below are practical, and for wilderness skiing, many of them are in the "necessity" category:

● rucksack—provides the easiest way to carry your supplies without impeding your skiing. Nylon or canvas ones can be had for two or three dollars, much less at army surplus stores.

● compass—may prove to be a blessing, but only if you know how to read it.

● extra ski tip—a "must". Made of either metal or plastic, it is easily attached and costs only three or four dollars. If you're a couple of hours away from home base and break a ski, it can be a long, tiring, chilly limp home on one good ski.

● plastic first aid kit—it should contain bandages or band-aids for cuts and scratches, tensor bandages for sprains, aspirins and salt tablets (for dehydration).

Injuries are not common in cross-country skiing, but the outdoors can be hazardous, even for experts.

● knife—a well sheathed hunting knife or all-purpose pocket knife is invaluable for fire making on the trail.

● down pullover—folds all into itself so that it occupies no more space than a small loaf of bread.

● map case or a plastic bag—to keep your maps (and this book) dry.

● wine skin—excellent for toting fruit juices and, of course, juice of the grape.

● vacuum bottle—a hot drink in the cold woods can be a treat for everyone.

● waterproof matches or a metal (flint) match—which is inexpensive and lasts indefinitely.

● candles—dandy for getting a fire going.

● emergency blanket—made of special insulating foil about the size of a package of cigarettes, it unfolds to blanket size.

● high pitch whistle—or an ordinary whistle in case you should get separated from your gang.

● flares—there are many types but pencil flares are the easiest to pack.

● glucose tablets—an inexpensive jolt of energy. Handy on the way home when you've gone further than you expected to.

CLOTHING

The clothing you wear will make a big difference in your cross-country skiing pleasure. Which doesn't mean a large fashion investment. On the contrary, the outdoor clothing you already have is probably quite suitable if you keep these few pointers in mind. Layering is the key, along with wearing clothes that allow free movement. Your body gives off an enormous amount of heat when you cross-country ski, so it is essential that clothes ventilate. Otherwise the moisture will be trapped next to your skin making you clammy and cold.

Checklist:

● long johns—ordinary cotton type, thermal or fish net. (Fish net underwear is preferred by many skiers because it creates an insulating layer of air between the skin and clothing.)

● tee-shirt—a cotton turtleneck long enough to cover the kidney area is best.

● sweater—usually a light wool sweater is sufficient, unless it's well below zero. In any case, it's better to have two light sweaters rather than one heavy one so that you can remove one if you get too warm.

● anorak—preferably windproof. This layer is important and it should be of a natural fabric which allows body heat to escape. Synthetics, like nylon, don't ventilate and a down-filled parka is too restrictive —and usually too warm. But you will appreciate the warmth of nylon when you stop, so it isn't a bad idea to pack a nylon jacket.

● knickers—preferably wool or corduroy. You can easily make these by cutting off an old pair of pants. But for beginners, any pants worn with knee socks over them so that they blouse at the knee. Even stretch ski pants will do if you release the instep and pull them up to let the knee bend freely.

● socks—one or two pairs. You may prefer a thin pair first for extra comfort and warmth, followed by heavy wool knee socks. Make certain they extend well over the knee to prevent chilly gaps where your knickers stop.

● mitts or gloves—your preference as long as they keep you warm but lining is helpful. If you're the cold hands, warm heart type, try down-filled mitts.

● a hat, toque, headband or bala-clava—whatever headgear keeps you warm.

● gaiters—similar to spats and very useful for keeping snow out of boots. They're easy to improvise by cutting the toes and heels out of an old pair of socks. You pull them on right over your boots.

● boot slip-ons—thin rubber protectors that slip over boots on wet, slushy days.

● sun glasses or goggles—whatever is comfortable and protective for you.

● beauty aids—wind and sun are unkind to skin, so if you're out all day it's wise to use lip balm or sun screen to prevent chapping or blisters, as well as protective cream or suntan lotion for hands and face. (Creams and lotions pack well in 35 mm film cans or snap-top pill bottles.)

Pack Extras
Although wearing too many clothes will make you perspire excessively (which may cause chills), it's absolutely necessary to pack along additional clothing in your knapsack—a heavy sweater, a nylon shell or down-filled parka, another pair of mitts, a scarf and a hat. The body cools off very rapidly when you stop skiing, it's usually colder in the late afternoon and should there be an unexpected drop in temperature or should you get delayed, you'll be thankful for the extras.

Jackets must be roomy enough to allow unrestricted arm movements and pants must accommodate the bending action of the knee.

CARING FOR EQUIPMENT

Follow these few suggestions for longer living, better performing equipment:

Skis

- Always stand skis on tails, base to base.
- When you stop on the trail for lunch, keep the bases of your skis away from the sun or the wax will soften.
- At the end of each ski day, wipe skis clean and dry. Allowing them to stand in a puddle of melted snow can cause eventual cracks.
- Ski racks can be useful for storage. It's quite all right for apartment dwellers to store skis on the balcony—but tie them down.

At the End of the Season:
- Scrape off all wax.
- Re-tar wood skis.
- Store in a cool place.
- Rack skis upside down in the basement if there's room.

At the Beginning of Next Season:
- Stand wood skis in the garage or place them outside for a few days before your first outing. Skis can

become brittle, so the moisture is good for them.

Boots

- Coat leather boots with a snow sealer before wearing.
- Repeat conditioning during the season, particularly if boots have been soaked.
- Never dry boots close to heat— they will crack.
- To keep the shape of your boots use shoe trees or stuff them with newspaper between wearings.

At the End of the Season:
- Generously apply boot conditioner to leather.
- Use shoe trees or stuff newspaper inside.
- Store in a cool place.

Clothing

- To prevent mildew launder or air out clothes and packsacks.

WAXING

The first rule of waxing is, don't let it intimidate you. Many people revel in its complexities but an equal number of very good skiers insist it is all very simple. They make it so, because they don't like fiddling and pondering— they'd rather be skiing.

Why Wax?

Although it sounds contradictory, the reason you wax is both so that your skis will stop and go. When a waxed ski glides forward over the snow, the friction it causes melts just enough snow to provide lubrication for the ski to slide. And when you press down, snowflakes grip the wax to prevent the ski from backsliding.

The kind of wax you use is determined by a number of factors including temperature, the shape of snow crystals etc., which is interesting but not vital to understand. (It's explained in a number of books.) But you should know this rule of thumb—*hard wax is used on cold, dry snow. Soft wax is used on warmer wet snow.*

Naturally there are countless kinds of snow conditions between dry and wet, that's why there are so many waxes between hard and soft. Although more advanced cross-country skiers and racers may use a dozen or more waxes, the beginner needs only three, or at the outside four: a hard wax for light powdery snow; a softer one for slightly damp snow; a very soft wax for wet snow; and, if you wish, a klister for icy conditions or wet spring skiing. You can purchase small kits complete with waxes, scrapers, corks, etc. Wax manufacturers colour code the various wax types, so as a beginner you should have one green, one blue and one violet or red. For best results, stay with one brand.

Preparing the Ski for Wax

Follow this checklist to ready your wood skis for their first run.
1. Ski manufacturers often coat the ski base with a preservative to prevent drying during shipment and storage. This has to be removed. You can scrape it off, use a solvent or ski it off. Check with your ski shop which is best for your skis.
2. Go over the base gently with fine steel wool and wipe off carefully. The surface must be smooth and

dry before you go on to the next step.

3. So that snow and wax will not penetrate the wood base of your skis, you must apply a sealer. This can involve brushing on a tar compound and warming it in with a blow torch. You'll probably do it this way when you are a real enthusiast because it gives a base that lasts all winter long.

But as a beginner, forget this. Instead, use a brush-on or a spray-on tar that air dries. Go easy with the amount, as too much tar will make your skis sticky. Cover all the wood, but with a *thin* coat. This base may wear down in places. Touch up where the wood shows through. If you want warmed-in tar (and this is the best), a ski shop can do this for about $3 to $5.

4. Base waxing, an optional step for beginners, isn't difficult but helps hold the final wax better. Use a special base wax (follow instructions on the package) or simply use your hardest (green) wax.

Waxing Made Easy

1. Before you decide which wax to use, judge the condition of the snow. Pick up a handful in your mitt. If you can blow it off, it is very dry snow and requires a hard wax (green). If it doesn't blow easily, use a softer wax (blue). If you can make a snowball, the snow is wet and a soft wax (violet or red) should be used. It can be this simple:

● dry snow (blows easily)—green wax

● dry snow (doesn't blow easily)—blue wax

● wet snow (balls up)—violet or red wax

● for very wet snow or icy conditions a klister is useful.

2. Apply wax in any direction, but evenly. Better two thin coats than one heavy coat. Cover the entire bottom of the ski, with the exception of the groove. Wax in the groove can cause icing.

3. You apply hard "stick" wax directly to the ski. Rub it in any direction, as long as you coat the bottom evenly. Special waxing corks are used for smoothing but an ordinary wine cork will do.

4. Apply the softer waxes with a spreader and smooth with the heel of your hand or an old leather mitt.

5. Klisters come in toothpaste-like tubes, are gooey and because of this can be tricky for beginners. Avoid problems by squeezing on sparingly, and smoothing out evenly with a spreader (better still, a blow torch).

6. Most waxes are easily removed. Use a scraper or a wax solvent, but blow-torching is by far the best method.

Still Easier Waxing

Some skiers consider that the best way around waxing is to use the Canadian-made *Jack Rabbit* wax. There are only two types—one for dry snow, the other for wet. Follow instructions on the box.

Waxing for the Perfectionist

If you wish to be quite precise about waxing there are numerous charts available which correlate wax, snow conditions and temperature. Or use the simplified table on pages 24-25 of this book.

Synthetic Skis

Synthetics may need a light sanding to remove the manufacturer's base preservative (see 1 and 2 under *Preparing the Ski for Wax*).

There are some new waxes on the market especially for synthetics, but you may have to experiment to find the right one.

Fishscales and mohair skis are waxless; obviously you don't wax them.

If You Use the Wrong Wax. . .

Ski for about 10 minutes before you decide whether your wax is right or wrong. Even the "right" wax may not perform correctly at first.

If you're backsliding, add another thin wax layer or apply softer wax under the foot only.

If your skis are "sticking" in the snow, you've likely put on too much wax, or it's too soft. Scrape some off. If they still stick, scrape all the wax off and re-wax with a harder type.

If your skis are icing, again, you've probably put on too much wax. Scrape off the ice, some of the wax, and cork the base.

Good Waxing, Better Skiing

There's no satisfaction like a well-waxed ski. It makes the difference between tagging behind and leading the pack.

Tricks of the Trade

● Wax at home if you are skiing close to home.

● If you're skiing a fair distance away, wax when you arrive—conditions may be different.

● Keep wax chilled—it's easier to apply. It's also easier if the skis are warm.

● After waxing, stand skis outdoors to let the wax cool down.

● Don't put newly waxed skis down in the snow. As wax is warm it will melt the snow, causing your skis to ice.

● When you're finished for the day, there is no need to remove hard wax. With a little touching up, it may be suitable for the next outing.

● Soft waxes and klisters may be completely scraped off between outings. Mostly because they are messy.

● The wax you use in the morning may not be suitable in the afternoon. If you have to rewax, remember you can put soft wax over hard, but not hard over soft.

● Always take your waxes with you on the trail.

● When in doubt about what wax to use, settle for the harder.

The proper wax for touring and cross-country skiing depends on the type of snow, how long it has settled on the ground and the moisture content. By selecting a number from each of the questions below, in sequence from left-to-right, you can identify a snow type. Waxes for that snow type are then listed in the table by manufacturer; only numbers corresponding to real snow types appear.

IS THE SURFACE . . .

1. Snow.
2. Ice, crust, corn or pellets?

IS IT SNOWING OR HAS IT SNOWED IN THE LAST FEW DAYS?

1. Yes
2. No

A HANDFUL OF SNOW . . .

1. Is very powdery
2. Blows easily
3. Blows with difficulty
4. Forms a loose clump
5. Balls up easily
6. Drips water when squeezed.
7. Is a mixture of snow and water.
8. Cannot be had—too icy

EXAMPLE: 1 1 1

WAXING CHART

Snow Type	Rode	Ex-Elit	Swix	Rex	Bratlie	Toko	Ostbye
111	Dk Grn	Lt Grn	Lt Grn	Turquoise	Silke (1)	Green	Special
112	Lt Grn	Green	Green	Lt Grn/Grn	Silke (1)	Green	Mix
113	Blue	Blue	Blue	Blue	Silke (1)	Blue	Medium
114	Violet	Violet	Violet	Violet	Blandingsfore (2)	Violet	Medium
115	Yellow	To Klis	Red Klis	Yellow	Klistervoks (3)	Yellow	Klistervox
116	Red Klis Yel Klis	To Med Tjara K	Yel Klis	Red Klis	Vat Nysno Klister (10)	Red Klis	Klister
123	Lt. Grn	Green	Green	Green	Silke (1)	Green	Special/Mix
124	Blue	Blue	Blue	Blue	Gront Klister (7)	Blue	Mix
125	Violet	Violet	Violet	Violet	Blandingsfore (2)	Violet	Klistervox
126	Red	Red	Red	Red	Vot Klis (8)	Red/Violet K	Mixolin (Klis)
127	Red Klis	To Med Tjara K	Red Klis	Red Klis	Vot Klis (thick) (8)	Red Klis	Klister
224	Red	Red	Blue Klis	Blue Klis	Vot Klis (8)	Blue Klis	Mixolin (Klis)
225	Vio Klis	To Klis	Vio Klis	Vio Klis	Vot Klis (8)	Red Klis	Mixolinvox
226	Vio Klis	To Klis	Vio Klis	Vio Klis	Skareklister (9)	Red Klis	Mixolin (Klis)
227	Silv Klis	To Med Tjara K	Red Klis	Silver Klis	Skareklister (9)	Red Klis (thick)	Klister
228	Blue Klis	Skare K	Blue Klis	Blue Klis	Skarvoks (4)	Blue Klis	Skare (Klis)

TIPS AND TECHNIQUES

One of the most encouraging things about cross-country skiing is that it doesn't require extensive skill or great athletic ability. In fact, if you don't learn any technique at all, and more or less just slide around on your skis in the snow, you can still have a lot of fun. However, the more proficient you become, the more you'll enjoy yourself.

The techniques outlined here are primarily to help the beginner get started, although there are tips for all skiers.

It is advisable to take some cross-country ski lessons. (For where, check the *Where To Ski* section which begins on page 46.) Once you develop your technique, you'll be prepared to ski on all kinds of terrain.

Starting Off on the Right Foot

Just as there's a left and a right boot, there's a left and a right ski. The outside edge of each binding and boot is considerably more angled than the inside edge. So the first thing you should do is place your skis on the snow with the angled edges on the outside.

Place your feet in the bindings, making certain the pins on the bindings fit into the holes in your boots. If your boots are the type without holes, make sure that your feet are pushed well forward in the harnesses. Then secure the clamps and you're ready to go.

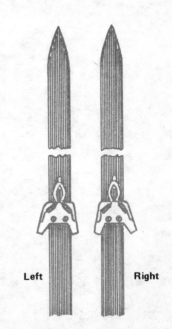

Left   Right

To get the feel of your skis, stand in one place and raise and lower each foot a few times. Then, with feet together, jump up and down. First with, and then without, poles. Next, without poles and with skis comfortably 6 to 8 inches apart, shuffle ahead through the snow approximately a hundred yards. Turn around and go back in the same track. Keep walking back and forth in this track until you feel you have a good sense of balance. Now try swinging your arms briskly as you walk. Move opposite arms and legs together like you're marching in a parade. When you've mastered this you can try gliding, which is the essence of cross-country skiing.

Basically, what you must learn to do is walk with an exaggerated long stride. You'll find the balance on skis slightly different than it is for

The beginner walks without poles, swings arms briskly

27

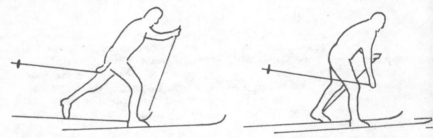

Skiing is rhythm and balance—kick, weight shift, glide, kick, weight shift, glide. . .

ordinary walking. So try this. Lift up one heel and push down and back with the ball of your foot. Relax, and let this movement propel your opposite ski forward. Now shift all of your weight onto the forward gliding ski. When the glide has diminished, press down to keep from backsliding and bring the trailing ski ahead. Push off again, this time with the other foot. Raise your heel, push down and back, and shift your weight (as you did before) forward onto the gliding ski. In short, what you are doing is pushing off with your back foot with the lifting of your heel, which drives your opposite ski forward along the snow. Cross-country skiing is rhythm —so keep practising. *Kick, weight shift, glide! Kick, weight shift, glide!*

Although you seldom think about it, in normal walking you transfer weight from one stationary foot to another stationary foot. In cross-country skiing, you are doing much the same thing except you learn to transfer weight from the ball of the stationary foot to the gliding foot. The action of the heel and the thrust back, called the "kick", gives you your forward motion.
If your skis backslide, possibly you are not pressing down hard enough at the end of the glide. Or you could be either kicking too late or too early. If you correct these points and continue to backslide, it's likely due to improper waxing. (See page 21.)

The Diagonal Stride

What you've learned up to this point

are the fundamentals of the diagonal stride, the classic cross-country technique.

To further this technique, bring your poles into action. Again, swinging your arms as if in a parade, plant the pole opposite to your forward ski about 12 inches ahead of your leading boot. Do this again with the opposite pole on your next step.

When you've perfected your diagonal stride, you will make a fuller extension of your glide by kicking your heel higher. This will lift the tail of your trailing ski up, leaving only the tip touching the snow.

The diagonal stride needs practice. Lessons may help you further, or consult one of the books listed on page 44. Perfecting this technique should be your goal if you want to enjoy the sport to its fullest.

The perfected diagonal stride

Turns

The simplest way to turn is to angle one ski out about 6 inches and follow with the other ski. Keep doing this until you're turned in the direction you want to go.

Some experts don't recommend the kick turn for beginners. But if you are a downhill skier you'll know it, and well co-ordinated persons can learn it without difficulty. As you become more advanced you will master this and several other turns—skating, snowplow, stem, parallel, wedelen—all of which again can be learned from lessons or books.

Going Uphill

Because of the nature of cross-country skis and the principles of waxing you can scoot up small hills with surprising ease.

But when the going gets tough, there are several things you can do. To go straight up, use short, quick steps, with poles slightly behind you to lock in your position. Your body weight should be slightly forward and your knees bent. Push with your poles, don't pull, and don't rely on your poles exclusively— you've got to work your whole body to climb.

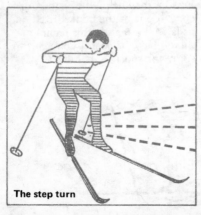

The step turn

Skiing uphill

A sure and easy way to climb up a hill is to side step.

A faster way up is to herringbone. But this requires strength and stamina. So the shape you're in dictates the way you'll go.

Going Downhill

The most exhilarating way to come down a hill is just to let fly, providing the downgrade is not too steep for you.

Once you're away, keep your weight evenly distributed on the heel and ball of the foot, stand fairly upright, knees flexed and one ski slightly ahead . Drop hands to thigh level and keep pole shafts back.

It must be emphasized that you would be unwise to attempt any reasonably steep hill without knowing at least the snowplow, both for control of speed and for turning.

The snowplow

Falling Down

And you will. Although you're not likely to hurt yourself. However, you should learn to get up with ease.

If you're on a hill, position yourself so that your skis are directly across the fall line. Otherwise, as you get up you'll start sliding down the hill. Plant both poles on your uphill side, place one hand near the basket and the other at the top. Pull yourself up.

Another method for picking yourself up, either on hills or flat terrain, is to lay both poles down in the snow parallel to your skis and use them as a platform to push up from. This is especially recommended if your poles are lightweight and you are not.

Some instructors encourage beginners to practise falling down. To do this, start skiing, then fall sideways. Just before you land, release your hands from the poles (that gets them out of the way), tuck in your elbows and cross your arms over your chest. This gives you the best protection in falls.

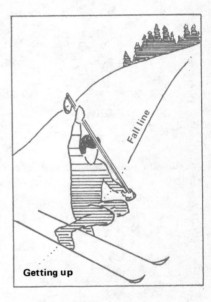

Getting up

Increasing Your Speed

To go faster on a gentle downgrade, double poling is the answer. Place both poles in front of you and push on them simultaneously until they are well behind you. You'll go faster.

Double poling will also shoot you over small bumps in a hurry.

Sudden Stopping

Should you ever get into a situation when you're out of control, don't panic, simply fall sideways. For a beginner who doesn't know the snowplow, this is the safest way to stop suddenly. Regain your composure and find another route to go if the terrain is too challenging. Whatever you do, don't sit down on the back of your skis to stop—that makes a toboggan out of you.

If you break a ski

Naturally, wooden skis are subject to breakage, especially if you ski in the woods where it's possible to stub your tip on a snow-covered tree stump or branch. That is why an extra ski tip is invaluable. But if you don't have one, a glove will help—slip it over the broken end and that will make the going a lot easier.

Crossing Roads

No need to take off your skis to cross a bare road if you're careful. Pick up each foot and place it down gently without sliding until you get across. Then check your wax to see that none has been scraped off.

Cross-Country Etiquette

Always let a faster skier pass. If you're skiing in a prepared track step aside. Should this prove difficult, give the faster skier at least one of the tracks.
When you fall down, tidy up the snow for the next skier, just as a golfer replaces divots.
Wherever possible, don't side-step or herringbone in a prepared track. Do this on the side of the track and the skiers behind you will have no complaints.
In cross-country skiing, "Track!" when shouted, means "Step aside!" At this stage of the sport only a few people know this, but yell it anyway and the rest soon will.

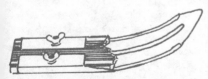

MORE THAN TOURING

Bushwacking and light touring offer abundant thrills and challenges, but if you're looking for that little bit extra, here are some of the added attractions of cross-country skiing:

Loppets

The world's largest cross-country skiing event, the Vasaloppet held in Sweden, combines both racing and touring and is conducted over an 85 kilometre course.

North America's equivalent to the famed Vasaloppet is the 100 mile, two-day Canadian Marathon held in February in Quebec. It attracts about 2,000 entries.

Closer to home is Ontario's Muskoka Loppet. After four successful years, the Muskoka has reached international calibre. This great day of family fun retains much of the authentic flavour of the Vasaloppet, even to the traditional "blueberry soup" served en route.

The course covers 30 kilometres—from Hidden Valley to Port Sydney on Mary Lake—and is open to anyone. An Olympic skier may streak over the course in two hours, but even if it takes you the whole day to complete it, you'll still have the satisfaction of participation. Tro-phies, awards and pine needle garlands are presented to winners.

In addition to the 30 kilometre course, on the same weekend there are 15 and 7.5 kilometre races for ladies, men and children, held between Port Sydney and Divine Lake.

For information on how to participate, write Muskoka Loppet, Box 1239, Huntsville.

Racing

Anyone who is interested in racing is advised to join a local ski club to take advantage of their race training program. (See the club listings on page 45.) If there isn't a club in your area that offers training, write the Canadian Ski Association, Southern Ontario Division, 4824 Yonge Street, Willowdale, Ontario.

A boy or girl of 14 usually starts training in the late summer and gradually builds up the workload, until, by 16 to 18, training is 2 to 2½ hours a day, 6 days a week. After competing at the club level, a young racer moves up to the divisional level, racing against other clubs in his or her ski division Next is the National Ski Team, then the Olympics.

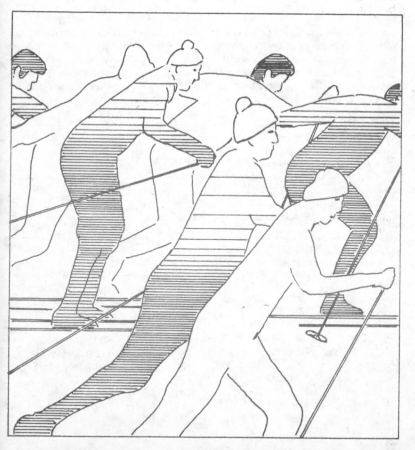

Instructors

Courses are open to those who wish to become cross-country ski instructors. Contact either the Canadian Ski Association or the Canadian Ski Instructors Alliance, 1460 Don Mills Road, Toronto.

Cross-Country Skiing Awards

The Canadian Ski Association sponsors a number of skiing awards for skiers who wish to test their ability against established norms. These tests are open to anyone, in other words, you don't need to be

Time Tests

Men	10 km (6.25 mi.)	Bronze	Silver	Gold
Class A	18 - 34 years	65 min.	60 min.	56 min.
Class B	35 - 49 years	70 min.	65 min.	61 min.
Class C	50 years & over	100 min.	90 min.	70 min.
Women	5 km (3.125 mi.)			
Class A	18 - 34 years	41 min.	36 min.	33 min.
Class B	35 - 49 years	45 min.	42 min.	40 min.
Class C	50 years & over	55 min.	50 min.	45 min.

		Boys Minutes					Girls Minutes		
Age	Bronze	Silver	Gold	Distance	Age	Bronze	Silver	Gold	Distance
7	32	30	28½		7	40	37	35	
8	30	28½	27		8	37	35	32½	
9	28½	27	25		9	35	32½	30	
10	27	25	22½	2.5 km	10	32½	30	27½	2.5 km
11	25	22½	20		11	30	27½	25	
12	22½	20	18		12	27½	25	22½	
13	20	17½	16		13	25	22½	20	
14	46	42	38		14	60	55	50	
15	43	39	35	5 km	15	55	50	44	5 km
16	40	36	32		16	50	43	38	
17	37	34	30		17	44	38	35	

a member of a ski club to be eligible. Some of the tests are outlined here; for more information contact the Canadian Ski Association office in your area.

Touring Badge: This is a recreational badge, ideal for family participation. It is open to juniors from seven to 17 years and adults, and involves logging accumulated ski touring distances to win bronze, silver and gold badges.

Other Touring Awards: After winning a Touring Badge for five consecutive years, the skier is eligible for an enameled necklace or cuff links.
If both parents and at least one child in a family win a Gold Badge for Touring during one season they will be eligible for the Family Diploma Award.
Any skier who qualifies 25 times for the Gold Badge will receive a Touring Plaque.

Time Tests: Non-competitive race-against-the-clock tests are for bronze, silver and gold badges— for men, women and juniors. Charts opposite show sample times.

Time Trial Ski Plaque: After winning a Time Trial Badge in either bronze, silver or gold, the next step is to win a Time Trial Ski Plaque. This involves winning your bronze, silver or gold Time Trial Badge another four times, passing at least one test per season.

Touring Badge

	Bronze	Silver	Gold
		Miles	
Men:			
18 & over	100	150	200
35 & over	80	120	150
50 & over	60	80	125
Ladies:			
16 & over	110	145	190
35 & over	80	110	135
50 & over	50	75	100
Juniors:			
age: 7	20	30	40
8	25	35	50
9	30	45	60
10	35	50	70
11	40	60	80
12	50	70	90
13	60	80	100
14	70	95	120
15	80	110	140
16	90	125	160
17	100	135	175

ENJOYING THE OUTDOORS

Exploring the quiet winter woods is one of the great joys of cross-country skiing and provides a great learning experience for children and adults. As romantic as the forest is, however, it can become a hostile environment for the inexperienced. Whenever you enter unmarked areas follow these pointers and good woodsmanship will become automatic:

● tell someone where you plan to go and approximately when you'll return.

● keep an eye out for landmarks. Places familiar in the summertime not only change when covered with snow but a trail can quickly be obliterated by a storm.

● take a safety bearing. Establish whether the road you used to enter the woods is to the north, south, east or west. Maps and compasses are useless if you don't know which way you came from in the first place.

● travel with a party of three or more. In case of a mishap, two can remain at the scene while one goes for help.

● even if you're keen and reasonably fit, start off with short excur-

sions, say a morning or afternoon. Then build up. Young children, in particular, lose interest and get cold if they're out for too long.

Treasure Hunts

Treasure hunts are great family fun, but they should always be conducted in areas you know well. Scandinavian skiers have been enjoying

them for years. Grown-ups can hide small prizes on the trail and mark directions to them with plenty of miscues, of course. Next time out, the children can hide the treasures.

Enjoying Nature

For extra fun on the trail take along binoculars, a camera and a bird book. Kids love discovering and identifying birds and animals.

Winter Camping

Camping can be an exhilarating winter sport but, it must be emphasized, this is not for the novice. How-to-winter-camp courses are available through many community colleges, Y's and outdoor clubs and such preparation is absolutely necessary before overnight camping is attempted.
For more information contact Mike Exall, Outdoor Recreation Dept., Seneca College, King Campus, in Toronto or the Bruce Trail Association (see page 45). Bruce Trailers regularly ski and camp out along the Bruce Trail, although accommodation is generally indoors.

Pack the Perfect Pack

If a sudden storm comes up it's easy to lose your way or at the very least get delayed, so each time you go out make it a habit of automatically packing these few items:
- a compass—know how to use it
- maps
- extra warm clothes
- an extra ski tip
- matches—wooden matches in a waterproof container (i.e. a 35 mm

film can), waterproof matches or a match flint
- a pocketknife
- a thick candle for starting fires (or newspaper and barbeque charcoals in a plastic bag)
- in addition to lunch, high energy foods such as raisins, dates, chocolate bars, nuts, peanut butter, orange juice crystals or boullion cubes.
- sweetened fruit juice in a plastic flask or wine skin
- a tin can—for boiling water
- a flashlight
- 50 feet of nylon cord—or rope
- ski wax
- a plastic ground sheet
There are several types of emergency kits on the market which are compact and lightweight and contain everything from matches to an inflatable bubble hut. Many are excellent, but your pack should contain *at least* the above items.

How to Keep Warm

- Jump up and down.
- Eat high energy foods.
- If your feet are cold, put on your hat (10 to 15 percent of body heat escapes from the head).
- If your hands are cold put your bare hands under your armpits, or hold your hands over your head then drop them forcefully.
- If you get frostbite on your cheeks, nose or ears, they will become white. Hold your hands on the spots until they disappear—and obviously, head back to base.
- To stay warm, stay "cool". Tension stiffens your body and makes you feel colder.

EATING AND DRINKING

Lunch on the trail is not only fun but an important refuelling stop. Here are some pointers for making the most of your outdoor repast.

- Hot or cold, functional or gourmet, lunch should be nutritious. You've probably burned up to 800 (maybe more) calories an hour during the morning's ski, so foods high in carbohydrates and protein are a must.

A substantial skier's lunch could go as follows:

sandwiches made with whole wheat bread loaded with egg, cheese, cold meats, peanut butter or jam;

plenty of butter or mayonnaise for extra energy;

fresh fruit—carefully wrapped, dried fruits—raisins, dates, figs, etc. and for dessert, a chocolate bar.

- Cold roast chicken or meat is also popular. Like fresh fruit, wrap carefully to avoid freezing.

- For haute cuisine on the trail try *Cross-Country Bonfire Fondue* (serves 2 to 4). It is cooked over an open fire:

1½ lbs flank or sirloin steak
¼ cup each soy sauce, olive oil and lemon juice
1 bay leaf crumbled

pinch of thyme
1 shallot, finely chopped

Cut the flank steak into 1/8-inch slices at a 45 degree angle. Or cut the sirloin straight across in 1/8-inch slices. Then cut into bite sizes. Use the rest of the ingredients for a marinade. Add the meat and refrigerate overnight in a plastic container and it's ready to go.

At lunchtime, skewer the meat on twigs and roast over the fire—it takes only a few seconds for medium rare.

Complement this with bread and cheese and dried fruit. By this time, a chocolate bar dessert will seem like a chocolate mousse.

- Cook-out hamburgers, wieners, steaks and chicken are easy and hearty. Or you could bring along a pot of chili, goulash or stew.

- Cookies and fruit cake are excellent high carbohydrate foods, but tend to be crumbly. So candy is more practical.

- If you want to be truly rustic, try your hand at authentic campers' fare—concentrated foods. These come in a wide variety from stew or spaghetti to biscuit mix and chocolate pudding. They're dried, packed

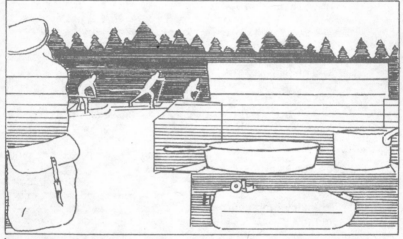

in water-proof packets and all you do is add water, and heat. Most sporting goods shops, especially those specializing in camping, stock these staples.

● Cross-country skiing is an especially fine sport for the weight watcher. It uses up so many calories that nibbles are free. A pocketful of snacks—raisins or candies—will keep energy up and you should burn off everything you eat.

● Even if you're planning a tumble-free day, avoid carrying glass containers or sharp metal objects. Knives should always be sheathed.

● A wine skin is the ideal drink container, provided you know how to use it. The *de rigueur* style involves squirting your "refreshment" at your mouth from arms length. Practise with water.

● When you're active and out in the fresh air, a glass of wine can sometimes affect you like two (or more). In which case, watch out for run-away trees.

FITNESS AND CONDITIONING

1. No matter what condition you're in, if you cross-country ski a couple of times a week you'll be in better shape for it. Cross-country skiing is the most physically exertive of all sports. Hardly a muscle goes unworked. It is four times as strenuous as downhill skiing, and racers burn from 1,000 to 2,500 calories per hour—more than competition swimmers, tennis players or distance runners.

2. For anyone who can walk, cross-country skiing is the perfect recreational exercise. The pace is up to you, but by thinking fitness all year round you improve your chances of being a better skier. It's the old story—walk to the store instead of driving, walk up stairs instead of taking the elevator and do exercises while watching TV or listening to music.

3. Any exercise that develops muscle tone and stamina and emphasizes breathing is particularly valuable for cross-country skiers. This includes calisthenics, aerobics, isometrics, yoga, lifting weights, cycling, jogging and walking.

4. Wherever possible, make the outdoors your gym. It's not only healthier but puts you in the environment you're training for.

5. Ideally, you should start to work out on a regular basis in mid-September for the upcoming ski season. Begin by walking briskly. Swing your arms vigorously. Breathe deeply. Concentrate not on inhaling but on whooshing the air out of your lungs to get rid of the carbon dioxide.

6. Next, start light jogging, gradually increasing your speed. A two mile jog two or three times a week, especially through undulating terrain, is a first-rate conditioner. Running up and down stairs is good, too. You are in fine form if you can do 15 flights.

7. When jogging, take your ski poles. Use them as you do in the diagonal stride. Take long strides. Concentrate on your kick.

8. Training on dry land with roller skis is great fun. Rubber tipped poles and a stop mechanism on the roller wheels allow you to simulate the diagonal stride almost perfectly.

Roller skiing —for racer training.

BOOKS AND SKI CLUBS

There are many books on cross-country skiing. Here are some that are currently available in Canada.

Cross Country Skiing, Hans Brunner and Alois Kalin, McGraw-Hill Ryerson, 1969

Cross-Country Skiing, Rob and Marcia Chickering, Anne Hicks, ed., Tobey Publishing Company, 1972

The Cross-Country Skiing Handbook, Edward R. Baldwin, Modern Canadian Library, 1973

Complete Cross-Country Skiing and Ski Touring, William J. Lederer and Joe Pete Wilson, W.W. Norton & Company, Inc., 1972

The New Cross-Country Ski Book, John Caldwell, The Stephen Greene Press, 1971

Nordic Touring and Cross-Country Skiing, M. Michael Brady, Dreyer, 1972

XC Cross-Country Skiing, Tobey Publishing Company, 1972

Magazines:

Ski Canada Journal, official publication of the Canadian Ski Association. 643 Yonge Street, Toronto, M4Y 2A2.

Ski Life Magazine, 702 Eglinton Ave. E., 416-423-5010

These are some of the cross-country ski clubs in Southern Ontario. Contact them direct for membership information.

Aberfoyle Country Club, R.R. 1, Puslinch, Ont. 519-822-5764
Beaver Valley Ski Club, 28 Upper Canada Drive, Apt. 215, Willowdale.
Bethany Ski Club, Bethany, Ont., L0A 1A0. 705-277-2311
Burlington Cross Country Ski Club, R.R. 2, Milton, Ont.
Caledon Ski Club, 3549 Palgrave Road, Cooksville, Ont. 416-277-2215
Camborne Village Ski Club, R.R. 4, Cobourg, Ont. 416-342-5323
Camp Wanapetei, 7 Engleburn Place, Peterborough, Ont. K9H 1C4. 705-743-3774
Caribou Cross Country Club, 393 Cummer Ave., Willowdale, Ont. 416-277-2021
Cedar Springs Ski Club, 77 Price Ave., Hamilton 43, Ont. 416-388-1433
Chicopee Ski Club, Box 154, Kitchener, Ont. 519-744-9462

Curlew Ski Club, Box 151, Bracebridge, Ont. 705-789-9998
Dagmar Ski Club, R.R. 1, Ashburn, Ont. 416-649-5951
Echo Ridge Ski Club, 25 Dorval Rd., Toronto 9, Ont. 705-534-1842
Eldorado 6000 Camping Club of Canada, 6 Pine Hills Rd., Toronto 5, Ont. 416-361-4729
Estonian Ski Club, 301 Riverside Dr., Oakville, Ont. 416-361-4729
Five Winds Ski Club, P.O. Box 93, Station F, Toronto, Ont. M4Y 2L4
George Brown College Cross-Country Ski Club, P.O. Box 1015, Station B, Toronto, Ont. 416-967-1212
Georgian Peaks Ski Club, Box 371, Terminal A, Toronto 1, Ont. 519-599-9926
Haliburton Forest Cross-Country Ski Club, R.R. 1, Haliburton, Ont.
Hamilton Chedoke Ski Club, 1072 Main St.E., Hamilton, Ont.
Hamilton Cross Country Ski Club, R.R. 1, Hannon, Ont. 416-692-3163
Hidden Valley Highlands Ski Club, Box 74, R.R. 2, Huntsville, Ont. 705-789-4350
High Park Ski Club, 819 Yonge St., Toronto 285, Ont. 416-921-2865

Horseshoe Valley Ski Club, 135 Fenelon Dr., Apt. 1011, Don Mills, Ont.

Huronia Cross Country Ski Club, 16 Fulton Ave., Toronto, Ont. M4K 1X5

Jack Rabbit Ski Club, Box 134, Cooksville, Ont. 416-274-2031

Limberlost Club, P.O. Box 1560, Huntsville, Ont. 705-635-2251

Madawaska Kanu Camp, 2 Tuna Court, Don Mills, Ont. 416-447-8845

Midland Ski Club, 632 Yonge St., Midland, Ont. 705-526-8233

Minto Glen Ski Club, Harriston, Ont. 519-338-2007

North Toronto Ski Club, 180 Eglinton Ave. W., Toronto 12, Ont. 416-481-5268

North York Township Ski Club, c/o Parks and Recreation, 5000 Yonge St., Willowdale, Ont. 416-225-4611

Northumberland Forest Ski Club, Cobourg, Ont. 416-349-2178

Pine Ridge Ski Club, P.O. Box 301, Oshawa, Ont. 416-576-1102

Seneca College King Campus Ski Club, Admissions Office, King Campus R.R. 3, King, Ont. L0G 1K0. 416-884-9901

SISU Sports International, 1111 Finch Ave.W., Unit 32, Downsview, Ont. 416-636-8606

Ski Bums Unanimous Inc., 102 Eglinton Ave.E., Room 4, Toronto, Ont. 416-488-5441

Ski-Mateers Travel Club, 120 Spears Rd., Oakville, Ont. 416-845-1561

Toronto Summit Ski Club, 8 Colborne St., Toronto, Ont. M5E 1E1. 416-368-1331

Toronto Travellers Cross Country Ski Club, (No Beginners), Box 400, Downsview, Ont.

Trent University Cross-Country Ski Club, Athletic Dept., Trent University, Peterborough, Ont. 705-748-1257

University of Guelph Club, School of Physical Education, University of Guelph, Guelph, Ont. N1G 2W1. 519-824-4120

University of Toronto Outing Club, SAC Building, University of Toronto, 12 Hart House Circle, Toronto. 928-4911

Voyageurs Kyack Ski Club, c/o CIST, 263 Adelaide St. W., Toronto, Ont. 416-364-3610

Woodstock Ski Club, Box 681, Woodstock, Ont. 519-462-2625

York University Ski Club, Physical Education Dept., York University, Toronto, Ont.

Additional Sources of Information

Bruce Penninsula Resort Association, Box 1, Wiarton, Ont.

Bruce Trail Association—Cross Country Division, 33 Hardale Cres., Hamilton, Ont.

Grey-Bruce Regional Tourist Office, P.O. Box 414, Owen Sound, Ont. N4K 5P7

Haliburton Highlands Resort Association, Chamber of Commerce, Minden, Ont.

Haliburton Wildlife and Forest Reserve, Box 420, Haliburton, Ont. 705-457-2455

Huronia Tourist Association, County Buildings, Barrie, Ont.

Lake Superior Division, Canadian Ski Association, 327 South Norah St., Thunder Bay, Ont., 807-622-2947

Muskoka Tourist Association, Box 58, Gravenhurst, Ont.

Muskoka Winter Association, Box 1239, Huntsville, Ont.

National Capital Division, Canadian Ski Association, Ottawa Ski Club, Old Chelsea, Quebec. 819-827-1717

Northern Ontario Division, Canadian Ski Association, 1353 Gemmell St., Sudbury, Ont. 705-566-6303

Ontario Cross Country Ski Association, Box 400, Downsview, Ont. M3M 3A8. 416-661-9900

Ontario Trade and Travel Centre, 145 King St. W., Toronto, Ont. 416-965-4008

Ontario Ski Resort Association, Suite 8, 15 Clapperton St., Barrie, Ont. 519-726-2940

Saugeen Highlands Association, Box 204, Owen Sound, Ont.

Southern Ontario Division, Canadian Ski Association, 4824 Yonge St., Willowdale, Ont. 416-226-1881

GREAT HOLIDAYS

There are a number of excellent ski packages available for cross-country skiing in Canada, the U.S., Europe and Scandinavia. To find out about them, check with air lines, government tourist bureaus, ski clubs and associations, travel agents or look in the ski journals. Individual plans are more expensive, of course but give you freedom to come and go as you please.

Here are some of the better places to choose from:

Scandinavia—the land of the midnight sauna

Norway: There is no status attached to skiing here—heads of state ski where students ski, and the night life is as much fun as the skiing.
Holmenkollen Days—a festive occasion at the site of the world's oldest jumping competition, just outside Oslo.
Birkebeiner—an open race for everyone who likes a challenge,—i.e. carrying a 12 lb. packsack for 35 miles, 20 of which are over open mountain stretches.

Sweden: Sweden is noted for "sunshine skiing"—and the grandest mountain sight is often the bikinied Swedish beauties on skis.
Are—excellent all-round ski centre, site of the Alpine World Cup finals in 1971.
Dalarna—site of the famous Vasaloppet from Salen to Mora where you and about 9,000 friends can enter an 85 km race. If you finish, you receive the coveted Vasaloppet diploma.

Finland: Ideally suited for cross-country because of the miles of gently rolling hills. There's a long ski season of dependable weather. Among the notable winter sports are reindeer safaris and reindeer round-ups.
Rovaniemi—way up in the Lapplands, near the Arctic Circle, but because of the Gulf Stream, it isn't cold.
Vuokatti—a year-round sports centre where there are a number of steeper hills for the advanced cross-country skier.
Near Helsinki—lots of good skiing at Aulanko, Laajavuori and Joutsenlampi.

Europe—something for everyone, at every price

There are a number of marathons held in Austria, Switzerland and Germany each year. Of particular interest is the Munich Marathon, a 190 km race from Bad Tolz to Munich.

Switzerland: Exciting outdoor extras and a night life that's as swinging in jeans as it is in black tie.
Davos—breathtaking, cosmopolitan, 25 km of trails.
St. Moritz—jet set sophistication, 42 km of trails and a marathon course.
Grindelwald—another jet set spot, shorter trails, with advanced trails a short distance away.

Zermatt—popular, lively, 8 km of trails with excellent areas in the nearby village of Tash.

Einsiedelen—renowned cross-country ski school, over 30 km of trails, near Zurich.

Austria: Every major downhill area has cross-country skiing, ranging from overnight camping trips to a morning's touring. The numerous winter walking areas and sleigh ride trails also provide excellent cross-country skiing locations.

Innsbruck—15 km of Olympic trails and 5 and 8 km trails for beginners. Big centre for all winter sports.

Seefeld—a chic sports centre and spa, 80 km of trails. Site of 1976 Olympic cross-country events.

France: Lots of cross-country in the lower villages of the Alps and les Vosges. Excellent cross-country ski schools.

Autrans—near Grenoble, over 100 km of trails in the area.

Chamonix—glacial skiing provides abundant thrills for the expert. A couple of small trails, too.

Italy: The Italian Alps and Dolomites offer many cross-country trails, some of which are quite new.

Marcialonga—a cross-country race in the Dolomites of 70 km.

Cavalesse—also in the Dolomites, courses from 3.5 km to 15 km.

Bruneck—in the south Tyrol, 20 km of trails.

The U.S.—land of hope and glory—and great skiing

The New England States offer superior cross-country skiing because of the rolling hills and sloping valleys between mountainous areas. Probably the most famous area is the Trapp Family Lodge in Vermont, but locations too numerous to mention are dotted throughout New Hampshire, Massachusetts, Maine, Pennsylvania and New York. Many packages combining ski weeks and lots of extras. Check with a travel agent.

Notable resorts in the west are Snowbird and Alta, Jackson Hole, Aspen and Vail, Ashcroft, Timberline, Sun Valley and Taos to name but a few.

Canada—land of mounties and mountains

Seemingly everybody's back yard is suitable for cross-country skiing and most downhill areas now have cross-country trails. The countless parks and conservation areas provide unsurpassed skiing through miles of quiet forest but some of the better developed areas include:

The Laurentians: Especially favoured for the Quebec *joie de vivre,* with excellent cross-country skiing in Ste. Marguerite, Ste. Adele, Ville d'Esterel and Mont Tremblant and Val-Morin.

Quebec City—Mont Ste. Anne, for the best developed trails.

Eastern Townships—well developed trails, scenic, especially Mont Orford.

Ontario: When the snow's good, the skiing's great all over the province. The woodlands of Southern Ontario, the Gatineau Hills across the Quebec border from Ottawa and the unspoiled wilderness of the Thunder Bay area are outstanding. See pages 49 - 79.

Western Canada: The Rocky Mountains provide unequalled cross-country thrills, the most spectacular being helicopter skiing. For the less-than-expert mountaineer, numerous trails cut magnificent journeys through valleys and plateaux.

Banff—11 km of trails at Sunshine Valley and skiing on the magnificent golf course at Banff.

Lake Louise—overnight cross-country trips on Skokey and Assiniboine trails.

Jasper—the Marmot Basin offers a thrilling network of trails ranging from 3 to 16 km, including the spectacular Spray Valley trail.

In the Rockies, some downhill lift tickets can be exchanged for a day of cross-country instruction and touring. Check with *Air Canada, CP Air* and travel agencies about Western Canada ski packages.

British Columbia: The Kootenays in the interior of the province, the Okanagan Valley and the Garibaldi Mountains, in particular Whistler Mountain just north of Vancouver, offer spectacular cross-country skiing. Plenty of good trails in the mountains in Vancouver as well.

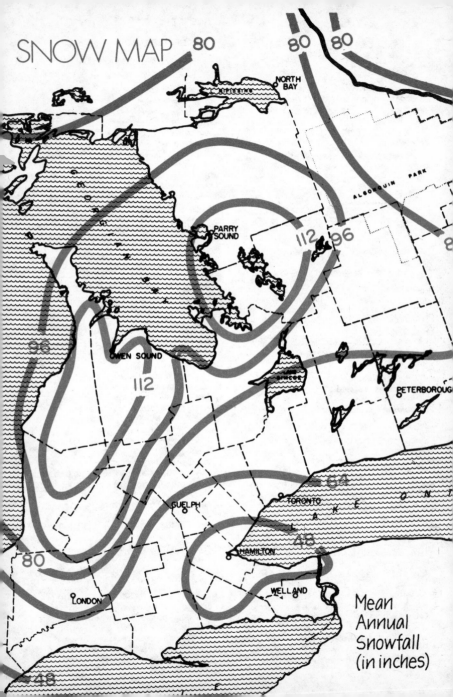

SNOW MAP

80

80 80

NORTH
BAY

ALGONQUIN PARK

112 96

PARRY
SOUND

96

112

OWEN SOUND

112

PETERBOROUGH

64

GUELPH

TORONTO

48

80

HAMILTON

LONDON

WELLAND

Mean
Annual
Snowfall
(in inches)

48

where to ski
METRO TORONTO

When there's sufficient snow, Metro Toronto skiers needn't leave town to find excellent places to ski. The parks are ideal. They provide a good variety of terrain and some have marked cross-country trails. Several offer lessons. Ravines, bicycle trails and walks are also suitable and some golf courses encourage cross-country skiing.

There are barbecue pits in many of the larger parks so all you need for a fireside picnic is the food. Wood is provided. Groups of 20 or more require a bonfire permit, phone 367-8188.

On the following four pages are trail maps of excellent cross-country skiing areas. Other good places are listed below:

David Balfour Park—Rosedale Ravine, Toronto
A 200-acre system of ravines in Rosedale and the Don Valley. Enter off St. Clair (a couple of blocks east of Yonge), at Rosehill Reservoir, or off Mount Pleasant opposite Carstowe Road.

Beaches (Includes Beaches Park and Woodbine Park), Toronto
100 acres of parkland along the shore of Lake Ontario, from Woodbine Ave. to Nursewood Road.
TTC: Take the Queen streetcar to any stop between Woodbine and Silverbirch.

High Park, Toronto
339 acres between Bloor Street and the Gardiner Expressway, west of Parkside Drive.
TTC: Take the Bloor subway to Keele.

Lawrence Park, Toronto
16 acres on the east side of Yonge Street, southerly from Lawrence Avenue.
TTC: Take the Yonge Street subway to Lawrence.

Marie Curtis Park, Etobicoke
On Lake Ontario. At 42nd Street off Lakeshore Road, west of Brown's Line.

Centennial Park, Etobicoke
200 acres with 4 acres designated specifically for cross-country.
Phone 626-4161.
TTC: Take the Anglesey bus from the Royal York subway station.

Highland Creek Park, Scarborough
In the Morningside area of this park, midway between Kingston Road (Highway 2) and Ellesmere Avenue, there are nature trails, picnic tables, fire pits. The Colonel Danforth Park section is a wooded area in the valley of the Highland Creek. Picnic tables, barbecues.
Phone: 367-8186

Thomson Memorial Park, Scarborough
2 km of cross-country trails. Lessons at a nominal charge. Washrooms, changerooms, and refreshments. Open daily. Phone 438-7411. At Brimley Road north of Lawrence E.

Downsview Dells, North York
In the valley of the Black Creek, enter from Sheppard West, west of Keele Street. Picnic areas, fire pits.

Rowntree Mills Park, North York
On the main branch of the Humber River, north of Finch Avenue West. Enter from Islington Avenue and Rowntree Mills Road. Picnic facilities.

Useful Telephone Numbers
For information on parks and facilities:
In Etobicoke, 626-4161
In Scarborough, 438-7111
In East York, 461-9451

In North York, 225-4611
In York, 653-2700
In Toronto, 367-8186

TTC Information 484-4544

TORONTO ISLAND

600 acres. Footpaths suitable for cross-country. Islanders offer free coffee to visitors. Skiing free. Phone 367-8186.

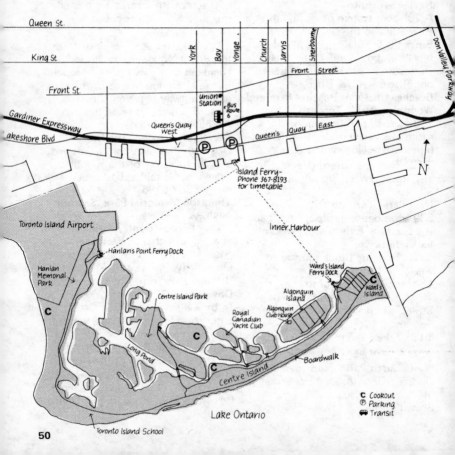

EARL BALES PARK
(formerly York Downs Golf Course)

160 acres. Marked trails. Rental equipment and lessons available. Ski charge $3.00 per season. Phone 638-5315

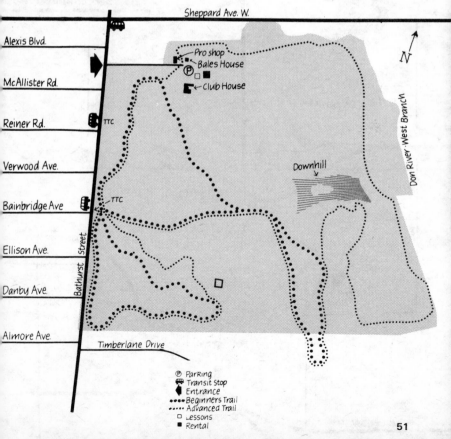

Sheppard Ave. W.

Alexis Blvd.

McAllister Rd.

Reiner Rd.

Verwood Ave.

Bainbridge Ave.

Ellison Ave.

Danby Ave.

Almore Ave.

Bathurst Street

TTC

TTC

Pro shop
Bales House
Club House

Downhill

Don River - West Branch

Timberlane Drive

Ⓟ Parking
Transit Stop
Entrance
•••• Beginners Trail
····· Advanced Trail
□ Lessons
■ Rental

where to ski
METRO TORONTO
continued

HUMBER TRAIL

Marked trails. Lessons in Magwood Park.
Barbecue pits. Skiing free. Phone 653- 2700.

Ⓟ Parking
🚏 Transit Stop
◀ Entrance
··· Trail
▫ Lessons

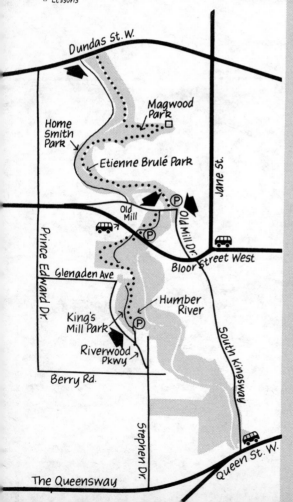

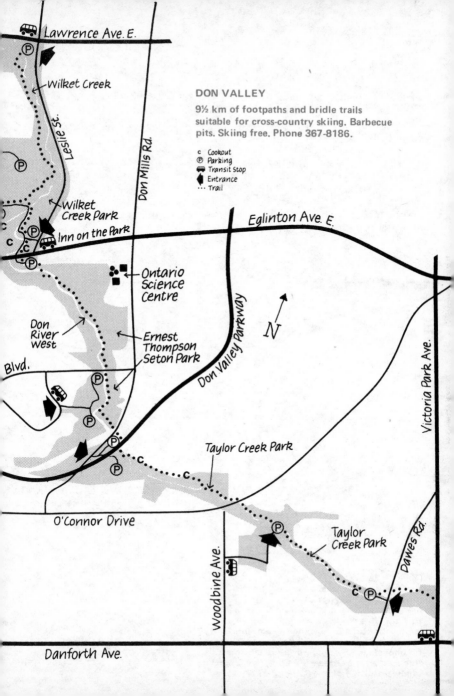

DON VALLEY

9½ km of footpaths and bridle trails
suitable for cross-country skiing. Barbecue
pits. Skiing free. Phone 367-8186.

c Cookout
Ⓟ Parking
🚌 Transit Stop
⬆ Entrance
··· Trail

Lawrence Ave. E.

Wilket Creek

Leslie St.

Don Mills Rd.

Wilket Creek Park

Inn on the Park

Eglinton Ave. E.

Ontario Science Centre

Don River west

Ernest Thompson Seton Park

Blvd.

Don Valley Parkway

N

Taylor Creek Park

Victoria Park Ave.

O'Connor Drive

Woodbine Ave.

Taylor Creek Park

Dawes Rd.

Danforth Ave.

where to ski
OTTAWA AREA

Within the National Capital area (a 30 to 40 mile radius) there are about a dozen developed ski resorts. Trail maps of some of these locations appear on the following pages. In addition, there are numerous acres of open land and endless miles of skiing to be enjoyed on both private lands and those administered by the National Capital Commission. For more information contact the NCC at 613-992-4321 or the Canadian Ski Association (National Capital Division) at 819-827-1717.

Further south, four miles east of Brockville, Maitland Trails is another good cross-country location with 27.5 km of marked trails over 1,200 acres. For more information write P.O. Box 89, Maitland, Ontario.

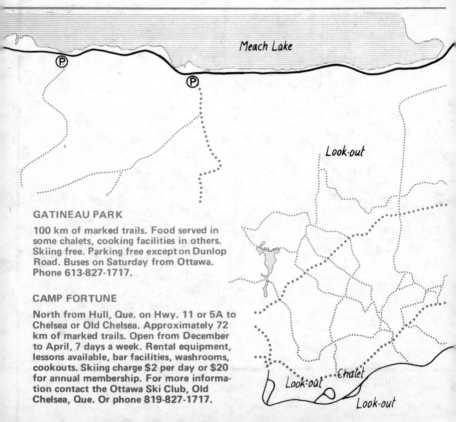

GATINEAU PARK

100 km of marked trails. Food served in some chalets, cooking facilities in others. Skiing free. Parking free except on Dunlop Road. Buses on Saturday from Ottawa. Phone 613-827-1717.

CAMP FORTUNE

North from Hull, Que. on Hwy. 11 or 5A to Chelsea or Old Chelsea. Approximately 72 km of marked trails. Open from December to April, 7 days a week. Rental equipment, lessons available, bar facilities, washrooms, cookouts. Skiing charge $2 per day or $20 for annual membership. For more information contact the Ottawa Ski Club, Old Chelsea, Que. Or phone 819-827-1717.

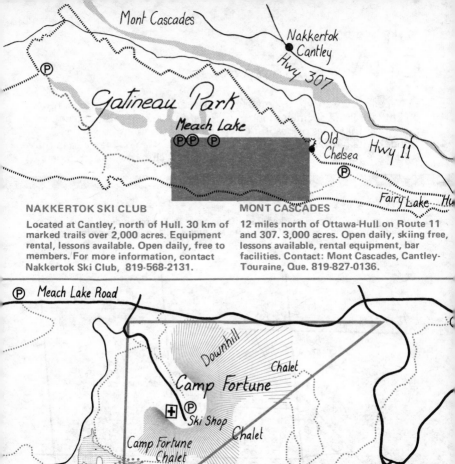

NAKKERTOK SKI CLUB

Located at Cantley, north of Hull. 30 km of marked trails over 2,000 acres. Equipment rental, lessons available. Open daily, free to members. For more information, contact Nakkertok Ski Club, 819-568-2131.

MONT CASCADES

12 miles north of Ottawa-Hull on Route 11 and 307. 3,000 acres. Open daily, skiing free, lessons available, rental equipment, bar facilities. Contact: Mont Cascades, Cantley-Touraine, Que. 819-827-0136.

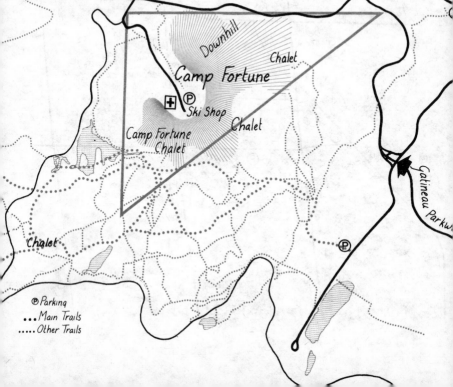

Ⓟ Parking
... Main Trails
.... Other Trails

where to ski
OTTAWA AREA *Continued*

In Nepean there are approximately 36 km of trails in six major loops covering 3,000 acres of beautiful woods containing an abundance of wildlife. A complete cross-country program has been developed to interest all skiers with instruction, clinics, marathons, movies and social events. You may also join the Riders, a club of volunteer skiers

STONY SWAMP

Approximately 30 km of marked trails. Open daily 8:30 a.m. to dusk. Skiing free. Waxing classes and tours with instructors. (Nominal charge for classes.) Phone 829-1510.

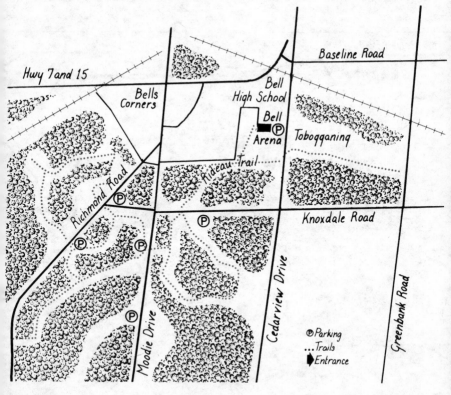

who help groom the trails. Trail maps are available at the Nordic Nook, the main office and the Sportsplex office. For further information phone 829-1510.

PINHEY FOREST

6 km of marked trails, challenging for young and old. Open daily from 8:30 a.m. to dusk. Skiing free. Phone 829-1510

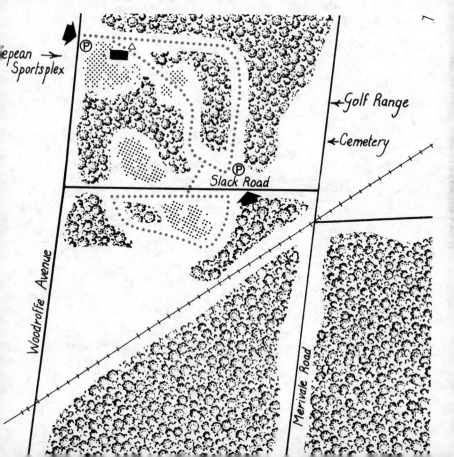

where to ski
OTTAWA

Existing walking and bicycle trails in the City of Ottawa have been extended and developed into a comprehensive network of urban cross-country ski trails. For example, Vincent Massey Park establishes the start of the Rideau River Trail. Marked trails along the river bank follow the bikeway system north to Cummings Bridge at the Montreal Road. The Ottawa River banks from Britannia Park to Westboro Beach also offer endless miles of good skiing.

There are, as well, downhill areas in the city that have good cross-country skiing: Mooney's Bay (see map below), the land near Rockcliffe Air Base, and Carlington Park. The Kiwanis Ski Schools operate at Mooney's Bay, Anne Heggtveit Hill in Carlington Park, as well as Blackburn Hamlet in Vanier and Maple Hill, Manotick. For more information about this program, contact the Ottawa Municipal Ski Council, the Kiwanis Club or the Ottawa Recreation and Parks Department.

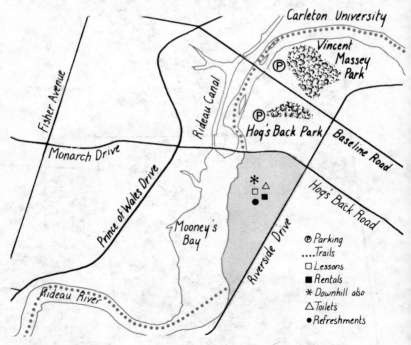

MOONEY'S BAY

Rental equipment. Lessons available Sat. and Sun. mornings 9:00 a.m. to noon. Essentially a teaching area but provides access to the Rideau River Trail. Phone 731-4684.

where to ski
ONTARIO

There is no end of places to cross-country ski all over Ontario and part of the fun is discovering your own favourites.

On the following **18 pages** are some of the places to ski in conservation areas and provincial parks and at winter resorts and ski clubs. Areas vary from marked and groomed trails to open fields and woodlands.

Each listing gives the location of the area, directions for getting there and the acreage, including the number of kilometres of marked and groomed trails, where applicable. (1 kilometre is .625 miles). There is also information on facilities, such as picnic areas, shelters, accommodation and an indication if lessons are given.

The maps on these pages show main highways but a good Ontario road map is a must for accurate pinpointing. As well as area maps, there are maps of particularly interesting cross-country trails.

Group excursions are arranged by many of the cross-country ski clubs and associations. Check the listings on page **44** for addresses and phone numbers.

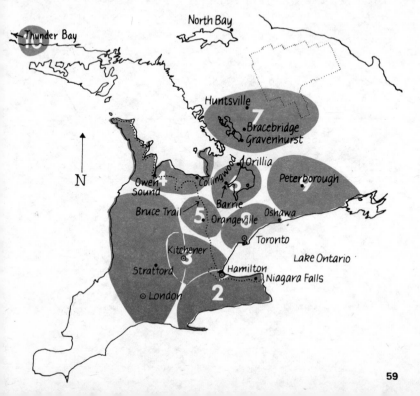

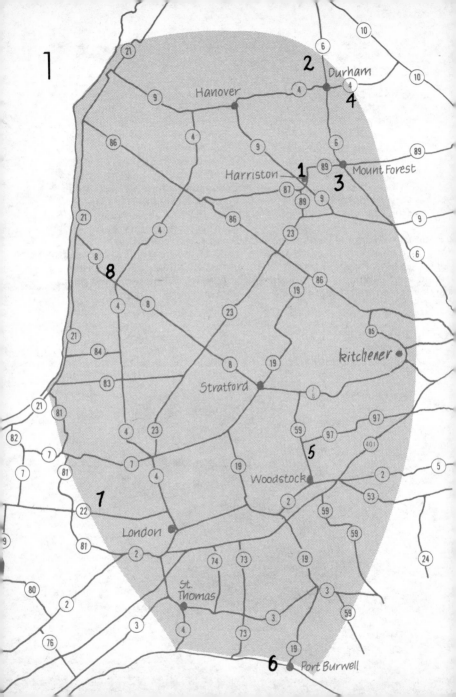

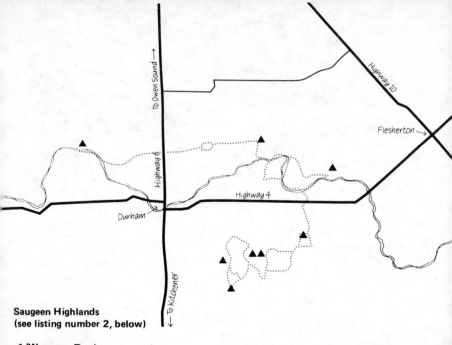

Saugeen Highlands
(see listing number 2, below)

1/Western Region

1 Minto Glen
3 mi. N. of Harriston. (Take Hwy 89 N. to County Rd. 2) 519-338-2007.

97 acres. Network of trails. Open weekends and holidays. Skiing free.
●△▲■C✳

2 Saugeen Highlands
Durham area. 519-369-3513.
Operated and maintained by 13 resorts.
Skiing free. 185 km of trails.
●○△■C▲→

3 Mount Forest Conservation Area.
Near Mount Forest. (Go 3/4 mi. S. of Mount Forest on Hwy 6 to Arthur Sideroad 3, then W. 1-1/2 mi.) 519-364-2251.

12 acres. Open daily. Skiing free.

4 Allan Park
Take Hwy 4 from Durham to Allan Park Village, then 1½ mi. S. 519-364-1255.

200 acres. Open daily. Skiing free.
△→

5 Woodstock Ski Club
8 mi. N.W. of Woodstock on Hwy 59. 519-462-2625.

30 acres, 5 km of trails.

Open Mon., Wed., afternoons, weekends and holidays. Nights Mon.-Fri. Charge for skiing.
●△▲C→✳

6 Iroquois Beach Provincial Park.
Port Burwell, on Lake Erie. 519-773-9241.

640 acres. Open daily. Skiing free.
△

7 Park Hill Conservation Area.
At Park Hill, at the junction of Hwy 7 and 81. 519-235-2610.

1,885 acres. 6 km trails. Open daily. Skiing free.
△▲C

8 Hullett Wildlife Management Area.
3¾ mi. E. of Clinton on Hwy 8, then 1¼ mi. S. on sideroad 10. 519-357-3131

4600 acres. Open daily. Skiing free.

---

legend: ● refreshments   liquor   △ toilets   ■ rental equipment
          □ instruction   ▲ shelters   C cook-out facilities
          ▲ accommodation   → marked trails   ✳ downhill skiing also

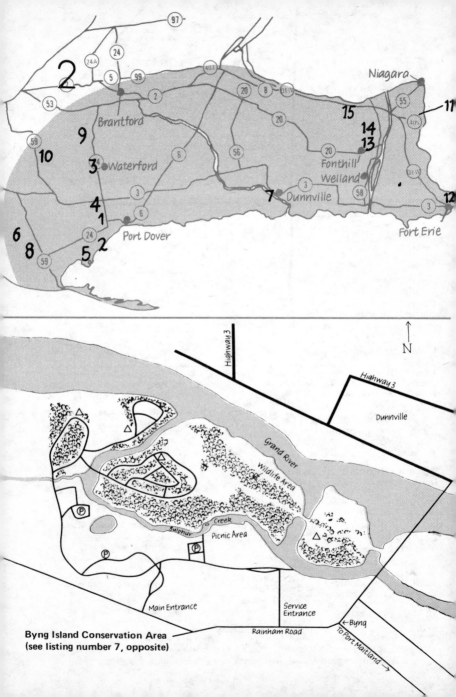

Byng Island Conservation Area
(see listing number 7, opposite)

1 Hay Creek Conservation Area. Near Port Dover. (Follow Radical Rd. for 3 mi. W. of Port Dover, then S. at Potash School.) 519-426-4623

100 acres. Open daily. Skiing free.
△

2 Fisher Conservation Area 4 mi. W. of Port Ryerse at Fisher's Glen on Lake Erie. 519-426-4623

122 acres. Open daily. Skiing free.
△

3 Waterford Conservation Area. 1 mi. W. of Waterford on County Rd. 2. 519-426-4623

257 acres. Open daily. Skiing free.
△ A

4 Vittoria Conservation Area. Near Vittoria. (Take Hwy 24 S. 4-1/2 mi. past Hwy 3 intersection to Vittoria Rd. Then W. 1-1/2 mi.) 519-426-4623

46 acres. Open daily. Skiing free.
△

5 Saint Williams Forestry Station. 15 mi. S. of Simcoe, off Hwy 24 S. 519-428-0330

800 acres. Open daily. Skiing free.
△ C

6 Deer Creek Conservation Area. Between Walsingham and Courtland. (Turn off Hwy 3 at Courtland to Hwy 59, S. for 9 mi. to County Rd. 30, and W. to Deer Creek.) 519-426-4623

65 acres. Open daily. Skiing free.
△

7 Byng Island Conservation Area. 1/2 mi. W. of Byng off Rainham Rd.) 519-621-2761

363 acres. Open daily. Skiing free.
△ A

8 Backus Conservation Area South of Walsingham. (Follow Hwy 59 for 3/4 mi. S. of Walsingham, turn E. on County Rd. 24 for 1 mi.) 519-426-4623

217 acres. Open daily. Skiing free.
△ A

9 Vanessa Conservation Area. 1/4 mi. S.W. of Vanessa on Brantford Rd. 519-426-4623

26 acres. Open daily. Skiing free.

10 Little Lake Conservation Area. 7 mi. E. of Otterville from Hwy 59. 519-426-4623

96 acres. Open daily. Skiing free.
△

11 Queenston Heights Park 6 mi. N. of Niagara Falls. (Take Niagara Parkway ½ mi. N. of Hwy 405 intersection.) 416-356-2241

150 acres (southern terminus of Bruce Trail). Open daily. Skiing free.

12 Upper Niagara River Marina. 5 mi. N. of Fort Erie on Niagara Pkwy. 416-356-2241

40 acres. Open daily. Skiing free.

13 Fonthill Ski Centre 1 mi. N. of Fonthill on Lookout Point Rd. 416-892-2631

100 acres, 3 km of trails. Open weekends and holidays. Wed. Thurs. nights. Skiing free.
● △ ■ A ✳

14 St. John's Conservation Area. 1-1/2 mi. N. of Fonthill on Pelham St. N. 519-892-2621

78 acres. Open daily. Skiing free.
△

15 Shorthills Provincial Park. S.W. of St. Catharines on Pelhamstone Rd. 416-892-2656

1200 acres. Open daily. Skiing free.

legend: ● refreshments ○ liquor △ toilets ■ rental equipment
□ instruction A shelters C cook-out facilities
▲ accommodation → marked trails ✳ downhill skiing also

1 Elora Gorge Conservation Area. S. of Elora, 12 mi. N. of Guelph, at Hwy 6 and Elora Rd. 519-621-2761

339 acres. Open daily. Skiing free.
△ Λ

2 Conestoga Lake Conservation Area. 10 mi. N.W. of Elmira. (From Elmira go N. on Hwy 86 to County Rd. 11 [at Dorking], and E. for 2 mi.) 519-621-2761

5,796 acres. Open daily. Skiing free.
△ Λ C

3 Laurel Creek Conservation Area. Near Waterloo. (Go N.W. of Waterloo via Columbia St.W., then N. along County Rd. 39 to Hallman Rd.) 519-621-2761

712 acres. Open daily. Skiing free.
△ Λ C

4 Chicopee Ski Club
5 mi. S. of Kitchener. (Take Hwy 8 N. from 401 to Freeport Rd, then go N. on Morrison Rd.) 519-744-9462

130 acres, 4 km of trails, access to Chicopee Conservation Area. Open afternoons and weekends. Skiing free.
● △ ■ □ → ✳

5 Pinehurst Lake Conservation Area. 4 mi. N. of Paris, 8 mi. S. of Cambridge (Galt) on Hwy 24A. 519-621-2761

285 acres. Open daily. Skiing free.
△

6 Shades Mills Conservation Area. In Cambridge (Galt) on Avenue Rd. 519-621-2761

350 acres. Open daily. Skiing free. △

7 Brant Conservation Area
At westerly city limits of Brantford on west side of the Grand River. 519-621-2761

424 acres. Open daily. Skiing free.
△ Λ

8 Christie Conservation Area. At Peter's Corners, S. E. of Dundas at Junction of Hwys 8 and 5. 416-525-2181

855 acres. Open daily. Skiing free.

9 Valens Conservation Area
At Valens, on Hwy 97, 5 mi. W. of intersection of Hwys 6 and 97. 416-525-2181

528 acres. Open daily. Skiing free.
△ C

10 Beverly Swamp Conservation Area. Near Dundas. (Follow Hwy 8 from Dundas W. to Bullock's Corners, take Bullock [or Brock Rd.] N. 10 mi. to Strabane, go W. for 4 mi. on County Rd.) 416-525-2181

1,063 acres. Open daily. Skiing free.

11 Chedoke Winter Sports Park. On Aberdeen Ave. in Hamilton. 416-528-1679

75 acres. Open daily. Skiing charge $1.00.
● △ ✳

12 Redhill Conservation Area. In Hamilton, on Stone Church Rd., E. of Upper Ottawa St., W. of Albion Rd. 416-525-2181

106 acres, 8 km of trails. Open daily. Skiing free.
→

13 Dundas Valley Conservation Area. Near Dundas. (Follow Hwy 8 W. from Dundas to Old Ancaster Rd. for 1-1/2 mi.) 416-525-2181

203 acres, 40 km of trails. Open daily. Skiing free.
→

legend: ● refreshments ○ liquor △ toilets ■ rental equipment
□ instruction Λ shelters C cook-out facilities
▲ accommodation → marked trails ✳ downhill skiing also

64

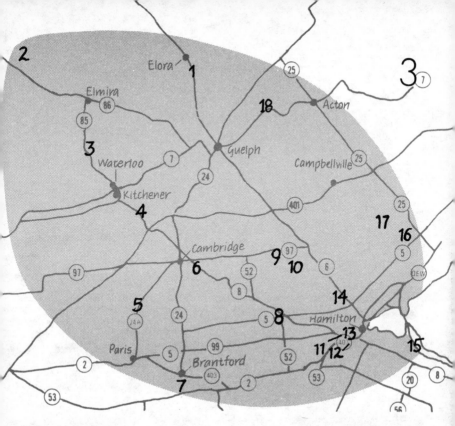

14 Crook's Hollow Conservation Area. Near Dundas. (Take Hwy 8 N. through Dundas to Bullock's Corners. Turn N. on County Rd. 4 for 1/2 mi., then W. 1/4 mi. on gravel access road.) 416-525-2181

37 acres. Open daily. Skiing free.
△C

15 Fifty Point Conservation Area. Near Stoney Creek. (From Hamilton take QEW to 50th Sideroad, E. on North Service Rd, to Base-line Rd. 1/2 mi. E.) 416-525-2181

99 acres. Open daily. Skiing free.

16 Cedar Springs Ski Club 7 mi. N. of Burlington (Take Cedar Springs Rd. off Hwy 5.) 416-528-5642

4 km of trails. Open Wed. afternoon and weekends. Ski charge $1.50.
●△□→✳

17 Halton Complex Various entraces on north south roads running N. off Halton Rd. & E. of the Campbellville Rd. 519-658-9356

890 acres, 13 km of trails. Open daily. Skiing free.

18 Rockwood Conservation Area. At Hwy 7 just S. of Rockwood, 7 mi. E. of Guelph. 519-621-2761

197 acres. Open daily. Skiing free.
△Λ

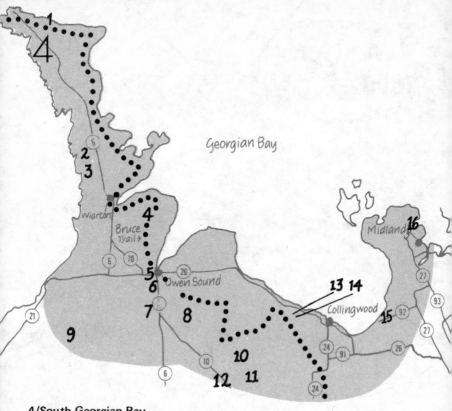

4/South Georgian Bay

1 Cyprus Lake Provincial Park. 35 mi. N. of Wiarton on Hwy 6. 519-376-3860

1,593 acres. Open daily. Skiing free.

2 Sucker Creek Conservation Area. North of Wiarton, 2 mi. S. of Pike Bay and 1 mi. N. of Howdenvale. 519-376-3076

300 acres. Open daily. Skiing free.

3 Rankin Wildlife Management Area. Between Red Bay and Oliphant. 519-376-3076.

22,000 acres. 20 km of trails. Open daily. Skiing free.
→

4 Keppel Escarpment Conservation Area. 6 mi. N.W. of Owen Sound. (Take County Rd. 1 from Owen Sound to County Rd. 17,

then go 4 mi.) 519-376-3076

2,000 acres, access to Bruce Trail. Open daily. Skiing free.

5 Pottawatomi Conservation Area. 2 mi. W. of Owen Sound on Hwy 21. 519-376-3076

300 acres, access to Bruce Trail. Open daily. Skiing free.

legend: ● refreshments ○ liquor △ toilets ■ rental equipment
□ instruction ▲ shelters C cook-out facilities
▲ accommodation → marked trails ✳ downhill skiing also

6 Harrison Park
Off Hwy 6 on 2nd Ave.E.,
Owen Sound. 519-376-
0265

114 acres, 4 km of trails.
Open weekends. Skiing free.
●△➤

7 Bay Motor Inn Ski Village
1 mi. E. of Chatsworth.
519-376-2700 (Toronto
364-3631)

500 acres, access to Bruce
Trail, 5 km of trails. Open
daily. Ski charge.
●○△■□✳

8 Rocklyn Creek Conservation Area. Near Owen Sound.
(From Owen Sound take
Hwy 26 E. to Woodford,
then County Rd. 18 S. for
9 mi.) 519-376-3076

256 acres. Access to Bruce
Trail. Open daily. Skiing
free.

9 Saugeen Bluffs Conservation Area. 3 mi. N. of
Paisley on Cnty Rd. 3, ¾
mi. W. on access road.
519-364-1255

350 acres. Open daily.
Skiing free
△

10 Talisman Ski Resort
1 mi. N. of Kimberley.
519-599-2520 (Toronto
364-0061)

200 acres. Open daily. Skiing free.
●○△■□▲✳

11 Beaver Valley Ski Club
2 mi. S.W. of Kimberley.
519-986-2520

150 acres, 15 km of trails.
Open Wed., weekends and
holidays. Charge for skiing.
●△■□C✳

12 Bell's Lake Conservation Area. 6 mi. W. of
Markdale on Cnty Rd. 12,
N 1½ mi. on sideroad
10. 519-364-1255

1300 acres. Open daily.
Skiing free.
△

13 Blue Mountain
6 mi. W. of Collingwood
off Hwy 26. 705-445-
0231

400 acres, access to Bruce
Trail. Open daily. Skiing
free.
●○△■□▲▲✳

14 Tyrolean Village Resorts
6 mi. W. of Collingwood
on Hwy 26, then S. on Blue
Mountain Park Rd. 705-
445-1467 (Toronto 534-
8452)

10 km of trails. Open daily.
No ski charge for guests.
●△■□▲➤

15 Wasaga Beach Provincial Park. At Wasaga Beach on
Owen Sound off Hwy 26.
705-728-2900

1000 acres. Open daily.
Skiing free
△▲

16 Mountain View Ski Hills
1 mi. N.W. of Midland. 705-
526-8149

7½ km of trails. Open
weekends and holidays.
Skiing free.
●△■□▲➤✳

Bruce Trail
A 450-mile hiking and
walking trail, the Bruce
Trail offers unique summer
and wintertime experiences.
Camping and hiking can be
thoroughly enjoyed for an
hour at a time or for splendid days without end, which
is why so many cross-country skiers are hitting the
Trail. Starting at Niagara, it
extends along the Niagara
escarpment, northward
through the Caledon Hills,
along the high land of the
Blue Mountains, north-west
across the Beaver Valley to
Owen Sound and finally, to
the tip of the Bruce at
Tobermory.
All along the Trail there
are shelters for overnight
stopping, campsites are
marked and resorts are within short distances, for those who desire
a few more creature comforts. Markers are well
placed and access is easy,
from most anywhere on the
Trail. Cross-country skiers
may become members of
the Bruce Trail Association
(for a nominal fee) to participate in day and weekend
trips in groups. For further
information contact The
Bruce Trail Association, 33
Hardale Crescent, Hamilton.

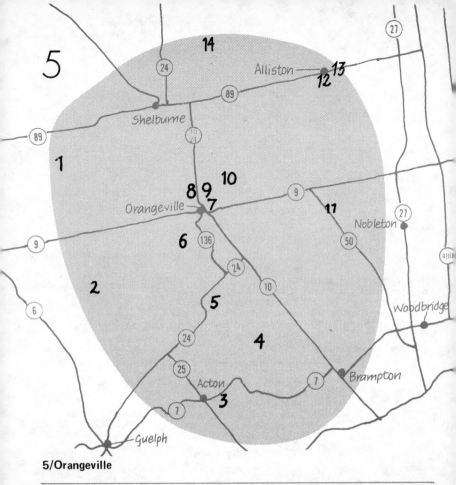

5/Orangeville

1 Luther Marsh Conservation Area. Near Shelburne. (Go 7-1/2 mi. W. from Shelburne on Hwy 89 to County Rd. 4, then S. for 3-1/2 mi. to County Rd. 15, then W. to Monticello, then S. 1-1/2 mi.) 519-621-2761

7,830 acres. Open daily. Skiing free.
△**C**

2 Belwood Conservation Area. 2-1/2 mi. N.E. of Fergus (off Fergus-Orangeville Rd.) 519-621-2761

3,281 acres. Open daily. Skiing free.
△**C**

3 Silver Creek Conservation Area. Near Acton. (From Acton take No. 27 Sideroad E. for 4 mi. to Hickory Falls, 1 mi. N.E. of Hickory Falls.) 416-451-1615

800 acres. Open daily. Skiing free.

legend: ●refreshments ○liquor △toilets ■rental equipment
□instruction Λshelters **C**cook-out facilities
▲accommodation ➔marked trails ✱downhill skiing also

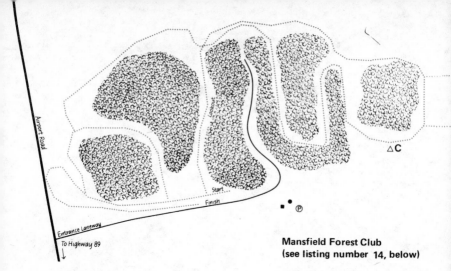

Mansfield Forest Club
(see listing number 14, below)

4 Terra Cotta Conservation Area. 1 mi. N. of Terra Cotta. 416-451-1615

310 acres, 5 km of trails. Open daily. Skiing free.
△C→

5 Belfountain Conservation Area. At Belfountain. 416-451-1615

22 acres. Open daily. Skiing free.
C

6 Wilcox Conservation Area Near Orangeville. (From Orangeville go S. on County Rd. 136 to No. 32 Sideroad) 416-451-1615

100 acres. Open daily. Skiing free.
△

7 Orangeville Conservation Area. Near Orangeville. (At intersection of Hwys 9 and 10 in Orangeville, take Hurontario St. N. to park entrance.) 416-451-1615

818 acres. Skiing free.
△

8 Hockley Hills Ski Resort 3 mi. E. of Orangeville on Hockley Rd. 519-941-4000

250 acres, 7 km of trails. Open daily. Ski charge $1.50.
●○△■□▲→✳

9 Monora Conservation Area. 1-1/2 mi. N. of Orangeville on Hwy 10. 416-451-1615

46 acres. Open daily. Skiing free.
△

10 Cedar Springs Ski Club Near Orangeville. 6-1/2 mi. E. of Hwy 10 on Hockley Valley Rd. 416-528-5642

2 km of trails. Open weekends. Ski charge $1.50.
●△□→✳

11 Albion Hills Conservation Area. 5 mi. N. of Bolton on Hwy 50. 416-630-9780

350 acres, 8 km of trails. Open daily. Charge $1.50 per car.
●△∧C→✳

12 Earl Rowe Provincial Park. 1 mi. W. of Alliston on Hwy 89. 705-435-4331.

750 acres. Open daily. Skiing free.
△

13 Nottawasaga Inn Near Alliston. (Off Hwy 400, go 7 mi. W. on Hwy 89.) 705-435-5501 (Toronto 364-5068)

135 acres, 4 km of trails. Open daily. Ski charge $1.00 (free to Inn guests).
●○△■▲→

14 Mansfield Forest Club 2 mi. N. of Mansfield on Airport Rd. 705-435-4479

800 acres, 33 km of trails. Open daily. Ski charge $2.00 adults, $1.00 children.
●○△■□∧C▲→

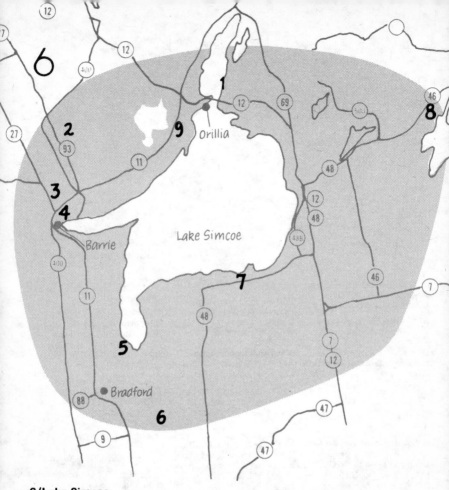

6/Lake Simcoe

1 Fern Resort
3-1/2 mi. N.E. of Orillia on
Rama Rd. 705-325-2256

Open daily. Skiing free.
●○△■▲

2 Horseshoe Valley Ski Resort. On Horseshoe Valley
Rd. between Craighurst and

Orillia. 705-835-2014
(Toronto 364-9509)

1,000 acres, 21 km of trails.
Open daily. Ski charge
$1.00 adults, 50 cents
children.
●○△■□▲→✳

3 Snow Valley Resorts
4 mi. N.W. of Barrie on
Snow Valley Rd. 705-728-
9541

8 km of trails. Open daily
except Mon. & Tues. Ski
charge $1.00.
●○△■▲→✳

---

legend: ●refreshments ○liquor △toilets ■rental equipment
□instruction ▲shelters C cook-out facilities
▲accommodation →marked trails ✳downhill skiing also

4 Molson's Formosa Spring Park. Barrie. (Turn off Hwy 400 at Essa Rd. Then follow Fairview Service Rd.) 705-726-2700 (Toronto 361-1407)

100 acres, 16 km of trails. Open daily. Skiing free.
●△■□→

5 Scanlon Creek Conservation Area. Near Bradford. (Go 3 mi. N. of Bradford on Hwy 11, then E. 1/4 mi. on the 9th County Rd.) 416-895-1281

400 acres. Open daily. Skiing free.
△

6 Roger's Reservoir Conservation Area. 2 mi. N. of Newmarket. (Take 2nd Concession Rd. N. from Newmarket at intersection with the Holland River.) 416-895-1281

96 acres. Open daily. Skiing free.

7 Sibbald Point Provincial Park. 5 mi. W. of Sutton. (Off Hwy 48.) 416-832-2261

400 acres, 3 km of trails. Open daily. Ski charge $1.50.
△ΛC→

8 Balsam Lake Provincial Park. 7 mi. N.E. of Kirkfield on Hwy 46. 705-324-6121

1,048 acres. Open daily. Skiing free.
△→

9 Bass Lake Provincial Park. 3 mi. W. of Orillia on S.E. shore of Bass Lake. 705-728-2900.

87 acres. Open daily. Skiing free.

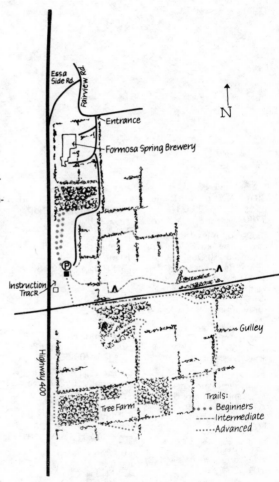

Molson's Formosa Spring Park
(see listing number 4)

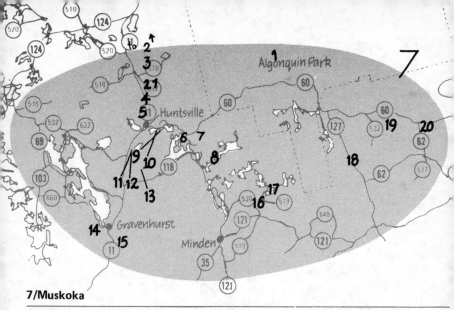

7/Muskoka

1 Algonquin Park
30 mi. N.E. of Huntsville on Hwy 60. 705-637-2780.

3,090 sq. miles. Winter access from Mew Lake Campground only. Open daily. Skiing Free. Parking fee $1.50. Winter camping facilities.
△AC
(only apply to Mew Lake)

2 Camp Wanapitei
Sandy Inlet, Lake Temagami, 60 mi. N. of North Bay. 705-743-3774.

Marked trails through Temagami wilderness. Open weekends or daily on request. Essential to book in advance. Skiing free.
●△▲→

3 Timberline
At Kearney (off Hwy 518). 705-636-5314

800 acres and access to Algonquin Park, 321 km of trails. Open daily. Skiing free.
●△▲

4 Echo Ridge Ski Club
10 mi. N. of Huntsville. (Off Hwy 11.) 705-636-5327

20 km of trails. Open daily. Skiing free.
●△■□→

5 Britannia Hotel
Huntsville on South Portage Rd. 705-635-2221

500 acres, 12 km of trails. Open daily. Skiing free.
●○△■▲→

6 Tally-Ho Winter Park
8 mi. E. of Huntsville. (Off Hwy 60.) 705-635-2281

50 acres. Open daily. Skiing free.
●△■□▲✳

7 Cedar Grove Lodge
7 mi. E. of Huntsville. (Hwy 60 from Huntsville 705-789-4036

100 acres. Open daily. Skiing free.
●△▲

8 Nordic Inn
½ mi. N. of Dorset on Hwy 35. 705-766-2343.

Unlimited acreage due to access to Crown land. 13 km of trails. Open daily. Skiing free to guests. Parking charge $2.00.
●○△□▲→

9 Hidden Valley Ski Club
5 mi. E. of Huntsville. (Off Hwy 60.) 705-789-4350

50 acres, 5 km of trails. Open daily. Skiing free.
●○■□▲→✳

---

legend: ●refreshments ○liquor △toilets ■rental equipment
□instruction ∧shelters Ccook-out facilities
▲accommodation →marked trails ✳downhill skiing also

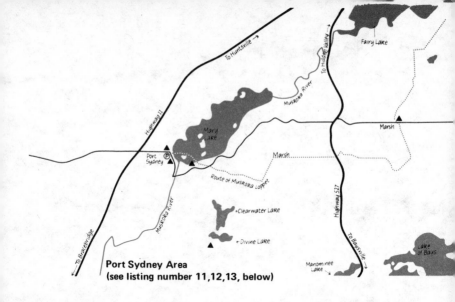

Port Sydney Area
(see listing number 11,12,13, below)

10 Curlew Ski Club
3 mi. S. of Huntsville. (Off Hwy 11.) 705-789-9998

150 acres. Open daily except Tues. Skiing free.
●△✳

11 Village Inn Apartments
12 Pine Lodge
Port Sydney, Muskoka. 705-385-2271

100 acres, 9-1/2 km of trails. Open daily. Skiing free.
●△■▲→

13 Divine Lake Lodge
3 mi. S. of Port Sydney. (E. off Hwy 11.) 705-385-2432

150 acres. 15 km of trails. Open daily. Skiing free.
●△■▲→

14 Muskoka Sands Inn
3 mi. from Gravenhurst on Muskoka Beach Rd. 705-687-2233 (Toronto 364-9612)

1,500 acres, 20 km of trails Open daily.
●○△■□▲→✳

15 Muskoka Village
10 mi. E. of Gravenhurst. (Off Hwy 11 on Muskoka District Rd.) 416-261-6215

Open daily. Skiing free.
●△▲→

16 Haliburton Forest Reserve
12 mi. N. of West Guilford. 705-457-2455

9,000 acres, 30 km of trails. Open daily. Charge $2.00 per car.
●△AC▲→

17 Sir Sam's Inn
On Eagle Lake 10 mi. N. of Haliburton on Hwy 519. 705-754-2188

100 acres. Open daily. Skiing free.
●○△■□▲✳

18 Lake St.Peter Provincial Park. 25 mi. N. of Bancroft off Hwy 127 on Lake St. Peter. 613-338-5312

2,000 acres. Open daily. Skiing free.
△C

19 Madawaska Kanu Camp
9 mi. S. of Barry's Bay off Dunn St. on Keg Lake Rd. 416-447-8845

50 km of trails in Madawaska Valley Reserve. Weekend packages, groups only, reservations only.
●△■□△→

20 Mt. Madawaska Ski Area
Between Combermere and Barry's Bay on Hwy 62. For information write Madawaska Valley Regional Tourist Council, Box 941, Bancroft.

1,300 acres, 48 km of trails. Open daily.
●△■□△✳

21 Arrowhead Provincial Park. 3 mi. N. of Huntsville off Hwy. 11. 705-645-5244.

2900 acres, 9 km of trails. Winter camping facilities. Parking $1.50.
△AC→

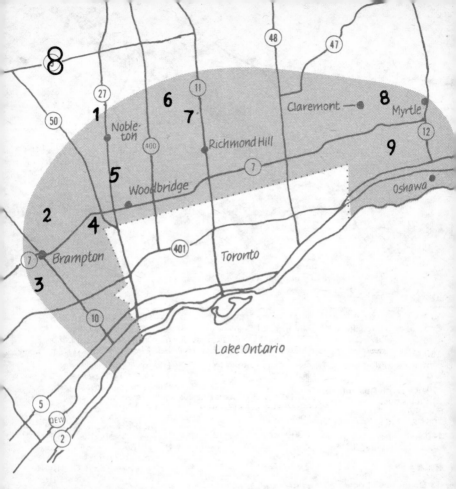

8/Toronto Region

1 Cold Creek Conservation Area. 2 mi. N. of King Side-road on the 11th Concession between Nobleton and Bolton. 416-630-9780

250 acres. Open daily. Charge $1.50 per car.
●△ΛC

2 Heart Lake Conservation Area. 1½ mi. E. of Brampton. (Go 4 mi. N. of Hwy 7 on Heart Lake Rd.) 416-630-9780

300 acres. Open daily. Charge $1.50 per car.
△C

3 Meadowvale Conservation Area. Meadowvale. (Go N. from Hwy 401 on Hwy 10 to Derry Rd., then W. on Derry Rd.) 416-630-9780

120 acres. Open daily. Skiing free.
△ΛC

---

legend: ● refreshments ○ liquor △ toilets ■ rental equipment
□ instruction Λ shelters C cook-out facilities
▲ accommodation → marked trails ✳ downhill skiing also

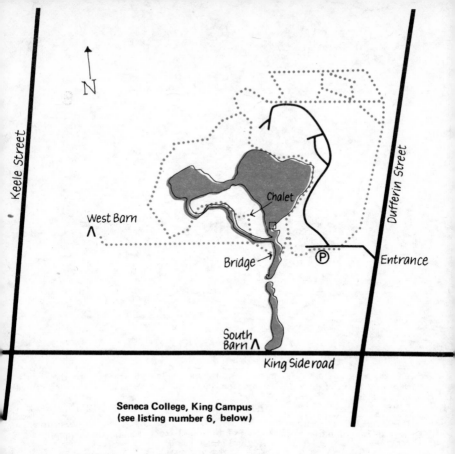

Seneca College, King Campus
(see listing number 6, below)

4 Claireville Conservation Area. S. side of Hwy 7, 1½ mi. W. of Hwy 50, on Conservation Rd. 416-630-9780

850 acres. Open daily. Charge $1.50 per car.
△C

5 Boyd Conservation Area 2 mi. N. of Hwy 7 from Woodbridge on Islington Ave. 416-630-9780

300 acres. Open daily. Charge $1.50 per car.
●△C✳

6 Seneca College, King Campus. On Dufferin, 2 mi. N. of King Sideroad. 416-884-9901

700 acres, 9 km of trails. Open daily, nights Fri. and Sat. Ski charge (incl. parking) $1.50 adults, .50 cents students & children.
●△■□Λ→

7 Aurora Highlands On Hwy 11 in Aurora. 416-368-1331.

180 acres, 15 km of trails. Open weekends. Ski charge $2.00.
●○△□→✳

8 Dagmar Resort 4 mi. W. of Myrtle and 4 mi. E. of Claremont. Near Ashburn. 416-649-5951

500 acres, 10 km of trails. Open daily. Ski charge $1.00.
●△■□C→✳

9 Greenwood Conservation Area. Near Pickering. (Go 4 mi. N. of Hwy 2 from Pickering on Greenwood Rd.) 416-630-9780

682 acres. Open daily. Charge $1.50 per car.
△C

75

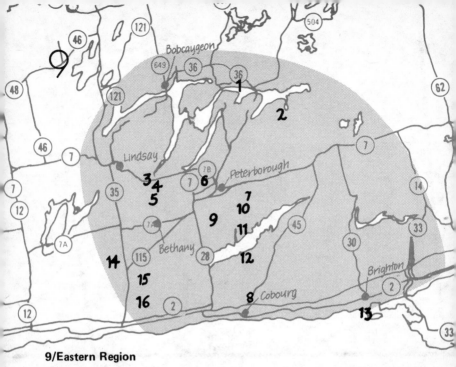

9/Eastern Region

1 Buckhorn Wilderness Centre. 4 mi. E. of Buckhorn off Hwy 36. 705-745-5791

1000 acres, 25 km of trails. Open daily, skiing free.
△∧C➝

2 Warsaw Caves Conservation Area. Near Peterborough. (Go 15 mi. N.E. from Peterborough to Warsaw on Peterborough County Rd. 4, then 2-1/2 mi. north.) 705-745-5791

645 acres, 10 km of trails. Open daily. Skiing free.
△C➝

3 Bethany Ski Club
2 mi. N. of Bethany. 705-277-2311

5 km of trails. Open daily. Nights Mon. through Fri. Skiing free.
●△∧➝✻

4 Devil's Elbow Ski Resort Between Bethany and Omemee. 705-277-2012

5 km of trails. Open Wed. to Sun. Ski charge $1.00.
●○△■□➝✻

5 Caribou X-Country Club 3 mi. N. of Bethany. 705-277-2012

120 acres. 7 km of trails. Open weekends only. Ski charge $1.00.
●△■□∧➝

6 Trent University Wildlife Sanctuary. In Peterborough on E. side of Trent Canal. 705-748-1247

200 acres, 8 km of trails. Open daily, skiing free.
△➝

7 Old Orchard Park
1 mi. E. of Peterborough off Hwy 7. 705-745-5251

50 acres, 18 km of trails. Open Wed. to Sun. Ski charge.
●○△■□➝

8 Northumberland County Forest. Off Hwy 45, just N.E. of Baltimore. 705-324-6121

4,000 acres. Open daily. Skiing free.

---

legend: ● refreshments ○ liquor △ toilets ■ rental equipment □ instruction ∧ shelters C cook-out facilities ▲ accommodation ➝ marked trails ✻ downhill skiing also

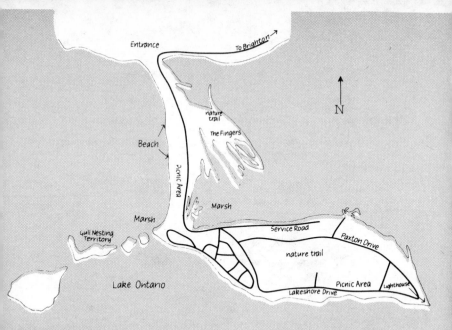

**Presqu'ile Provincial Park
(see listing number 13, below)**

9 Squirrel Creek Conservation Area. Near Peterborough. (Go 12 mi. S. of Peterborough on Hwy 28, then 2 mi. E. on Durham and Northumberland County Rd. 13.) 705-745-5791

275 acres, 2.5 km of trails. Open daily. Skiing free.
△ →

10 Hope Mill Conservation Area. Near Peterborough. (Take Hwy 7 E. from Peterborough for 6 mi. to County Rd. 34. Turn S. for 2-1/2 mi. then take access road E. 1/2 mi.) 705-745-5791.

122 acres. Open daily. Skiing free.
△

11 Serpent Mounds Provincial Park. On W. shore of Rice Lake near Keene. (Go 7 mi. E. of Peterborough on Hwy 7, then 8 mi. S. on Peterborough Rd. through Keene.) 705-324-6121

70 acres. Open daily. Skiing free.
△C

12 Camborne Village Ski Club. N. of Cobourg in Camborne. 416-342-5323

30 acres, 6 km of trails. Day skiing weekends and Tues. and Thurs. Night skiing Tues., Wed., Thurs. Ski charge.
●△

13 Presqu'ile Provincial Park 2 mi. S. of Brighton. 613-475-2204

2,000 acres. Open daily. Skiing free.
△C

14 Mosport Cross-Country Ski Park. 12 mi. N. of Bowmanville via Liberty St. 416-781-6626

700 acres. Open weekends and holidays. Ski charge $1.50.
●△■□ →

15 Durham County Forest. Near Newcastle. In Clarke Township at the junction of Hwy. 35 and 115. 705-324-6121

2,000 acres. Open daily. Skiing free.

16 Kendal Recreation Area. 5 mi. E of Kirby on County Rd. 9. 416-723-4341

800 acres. Open Daily. Skiing free.

10/Thunder Bay

Thunder Bay is an ideal place for cross-country skiing because of the vast suitable terrain, most of which is scenic, unspoiled wilderness. In addition, there are five major downhill ski areas with cross-country facilities offering an excellent range of beginner and expert trails.

Thunder Bay is also the training centre for the Canadian Olympic Jumping Team.

Loch Lomond—300 acres with 3 and 6 km of marked trails. Open daily. Skiing free. Restaurant and bar facilities.

CANDY MOUNTAIN
436 acres. 8 km (inner loop) and 9½ km (outer loop) of marked trails. Open daily except Monday. Skiing free (nominal charge for ski maps). Restaurant and bar facilities. Lessons available. Phone 577-6033

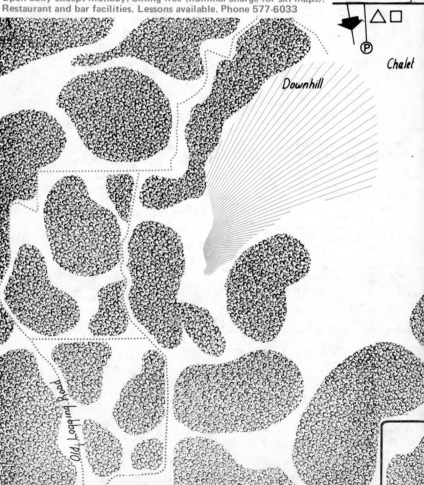

Thunder Bay →

Chalet

Downhill

Old Logging Road

Rental equipment. Lessons available. Phone 577-8926.

Mount Baldy—Hwy. 800, two miles north of Expressway. Three marked trails: 5, 8 and 11 km. Open Wednesday to Sunday and all holidays. Skiing free. Restaurant. Rental equipment. Lessons available. Phone 683-6981

Mount Norway—8 mi. west of Thunder Bay on Hwy. 61. Two trails—approx. 2.5 and 3 km. Open daily. Skiing free (nominal charge for trail maps). Restaurant. Lessons available. Phone 577-8813

Mount McKay—Hwy. 61 at Mountain Rd. Cross-country proposed for 1975. Open daily, Tues., Wed., Thurs., Fri. nights. Phone 623-6822.

CENTENNIAL PARK

3 International racing tracks—2.5 km, 5 km and 10 km and a 10 km touring trail. Lessons available. Skiing free. Open daily. Restaurant.

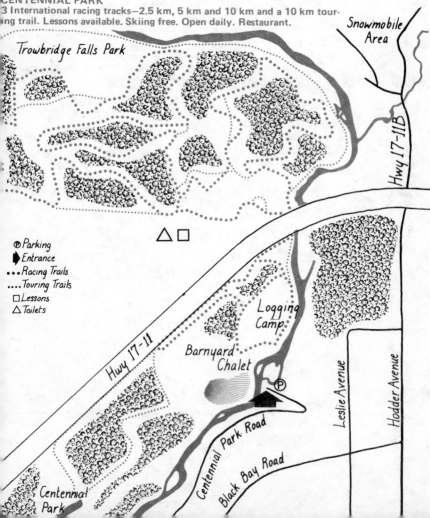

Snowmobile Area

Trowbridge Falls Park

Hwy 17-11B

⊕ Parking
◢ Entrance
••• Racing Trails
···· Touring Trails
□ Lessons
△ Toilets

Logging Camp

Hwy 17-11

Barnyard Chalet

ⓟ

Leslie Avenue

Hodder Avenue

Centennial Park Road

Black Bay Road

Centennial Park